Adiga's
hite Tiger
reakish Booker

Aravind Adiga's *The White Tiger*
A Freakish Booker

Sudhir K. Arora

AUTHORSPRESS
Publishers of Scholarly Books

Worldwide Circulation through Authorspress Global Network

First Published 2011
by
Authorspress

Editorial
Q-2A Hauz Khas Enclave
New Delhi-110 016
e-mail: authorspress@yahoo.com

Marketing
E-35/103, Jawahar Park
Laxmi Nagar, Delhi-110 092
e-mail: authorspress@yahoo.com

Aravind Adiga's *The White Tiger:* A Freakish Booker
ISBN 978-81-7273-583-8

Printed in India at Tarun Offset, Delhi.

Oh Lord Sai
You are the whole manifestation,
the Infinite Grace constantly at work
to bring the world out of its misery

—*Sudarshan Kcherry*

Poetical Portrait of Aravind Adiga

O White Tiger! You were named so
because you were different from others.
You learned how to pounce from the celebrated Eastern and Western masters.
But, just for the belly
you betrayed the conscience and entered the yellow jungle
where you are resting while waking thinking that others are sleeping.
Skin-whitening creams can whiten the black mask for your supremacy
in the white and yellow jungles
but never whiten your fresh blood stained hand.
You sharpened your paws on the foreign slab
gripped the golden bird and wounded her wings.
Even then, she embraced you and offered her haven.
You crushed her body to gratify the butcher in you.
She swallowed her tears to make you cheerful
with the hope that one day you will come out of the foreign jungle
and apply the ointment on her injured wings
so that she may show the world her strength of flight.
How the red lotus entered the red mud is a mystery to the bird.
O Indian tiger! You are an original listener.
Why did you forget to listen to your inner self?
The way you roar makes her proud but what you roar shocks her.
Even then, she is your mother who will not blame you
Because she knows that tiger whether white or black
becomes silent before the Tiger of tigers—Death
who comes and takes all to the unknown territory where nothing is for sale.

Contents

1
A Snapshot

Any action that takes to the path of progress is the right action. What counts is success, not the means which may be fair or foul provided that they bring success. The touchstone of success makes foul fair and fair foul. It becomes a part of slavish imitation that a literary artist, if he bags a prize or an award from a foreign country, is honoured in his native country and considered the real hero for bringing name to the country. The prize is taken into consideration, not the way he got it. Naipaul sells the nakedness of India and brings prizes and awards in return. Even then, he is embraced by the Indians not because of his displaying India's nakedness but because of his ancestors who lived in India. How far such a literary artist will be tolerated leaves a question mark on the mentality of the Indians who, with the feeling of cosmopolitanism, embrace everyone and forgive in spite of knowing the wickedness.

The spirit of Naipaul has entered Aravind Adiga who also uncovers Mother India on the Western stage and demonstrates her body infected with diseases like poverty and corruption to the extent that the West becomes lusty enough to make her 'Other', and for this he is awarded with the Booker Prize so that many more white tigers from India may follow him and help the West in proving the superiority of the Occident over the Orient. The equation that 'crime results in punishment' is changed into a new equation which recommends that 'crime results in prizes and awards'. "Kill enough people and they will put up bronze statues to you near Parliament House in Delhi" (318).

If Adiga has committed the crime of presenting the derogatory image of India on the Western ramp, he has done nothing wrong because he has followed the new equation. Through Balram Halwai in *The White Tiger*, he has given the new mantra of success to the Indians, particularly the subalterns, of whom he is the Messiah. The new mantra is: Murder, steal and enjoy life with wine, women and wealth. Balram, who represents the weaker sections or the *dalits,* does not feel any hesitation in leaving his family members to the point of their murders for realising his ambition of becoming rich and a master. How Balram Halwai can be a genuine well-wisher or representative of the subalterns is beyond understanding. Adiga knows better.

Now, come to the family background of Aravind Adiga, a journalist by profession and a novelist by passion. Being well equipped with the dual citizenship of India and Australia, the October 23, 1974 born Adiga, who hails from Madras, presently known as Chennai, is the son of the Kannadiga parents K. Madhava and Usha Adiga from Mangalore, Karntaka. The ground of Mangalore saw him growing up and studying at Canara High School. After securing first rank in SSLC in 1990 from St. Aloysius High School, with his family he moved to Sydney (Australia) where he studied at James Ruse Agricultural High School. In 1997, he graduated as salutatorian from Columbia University in New York. From Columbia, he moved to Magdalen College, Oxford where he studied under the guidance of Hermione Lee and others. Presently he lives in Mumbai.

The Financial Times provided him ground for the beginning of his career in journalism as a financial journalist. Then, he made his journalistic roots firm through covering the stock market, investment, interviews, reviews etc. that appeared in *Money*, *The Wall Street Journal*, *The Second Circle*, an online literary review and other significant journals and newspapers. Then, *Time* hired him as a South Asia correspondent for three years. Then, he opted for being a freelance writer. The freelance period resulted in the making of *The White Tiger*, the debut novel for which he won the Man Booker Prize for fiction in

2008. His second book, titled *Between the Assassinations* (2008), contains 12 interlinked short stories. His short stories, "The Sultan's Battery" (*The Guardian*, October 18 2008, online text), "Smack" (*The Sunday Times*, November 16 2008, online text), "Last Christmas in Bandra" (*The Times*, December 19 2008, online text) and "*The Elephant*" (The New Yorker, January 26 2009) are worthreading and reveal his creative potential. His new novel, titled *Last Man in the Tower,* is scheduled to be released by HarperCollins India in 2011.

This is the background with which Adiga has appeared in the domain of Indian Fiction in English. The rich English background qualifies him for novel writing in English. His authenticity in writing in English remains unchallenged. What makes his integrity doubtful is not the manner but the matter that he dishes out in the English plates meant for the English-reading people, particularly the Western reader. The body—the life of the poor people from the village—is Indian but its spirit is Western. Again, the discourse related to writing: "Who writes and for whom?" becomes alive.

Adiga is also interrogated from this point of view. Who writes? Adiga. Is he an Indian? Yes, he is. But, he is also an Australian. What does he write? He writes on India and her people. Does he know them? The answer is not clear. Who knows the land better—a farmer or a tourist? Certainly, it is a farmer. But, it does not mean that a tourist cannot write. The difference is not of kind but of degree. A farmer has an emotional relation with his land. The tourist is not attached to the land the way a farmer is.

Does a stay of few days in a village provide the sufficient material for writing a novel on the village life? Does the stay make him able to peep into the very spirit of the villagers? Will he not be prejudiced in the depiction of the village? All such questions are debatable and evoke different reactions and responses. There is one ridiculous response that has come to the surface. It is that if one who wishes to portray the Indian life one should visit the developed countries of the West. Then, he will judge the real condition better and offer an authentic commentary. But, again, it gives birth to some more questions.

Go to the foreign countries to write better and be authentic about India. What a nasty logic! India from the Western point of view is different from India from the Indian point of view. The reality is that when countries differ, angles differ, geographies differ, cultures differ, so circumstances differ, so how can one pass judgment on the basis of the country other than the native one? There is no end to such discussions but one thing that is not debatable is that a writer who wishes to write on India and her people is supposed to feel like an Indian first. If he does so, the narration will be authentic. If Indian writers do not have their connection and write about rural India, their depictions become biased. How can one, who is rootless, talk about roots, particularly village roots? Adiga is an Indian with the Western spirit. Here lies his authenticity in peril because of his Western specs through which he sees India.

A postmodernist text offers various interpretations. A man's interpretation may be right from his point of view but not from other men's and vice versa. Both are right but are wrong from each other's viewpoints. God created the world and left the people. Now, people live in different ways which may differ from one another. God cannot be held responsible for their way of living. One cannot forget Hamlet for whom goodness or badness does not depend on the thing but on the thinking process. The same applies to the creative writer who creates a fictional world and gets praise for his creation but does not agree with the characters of his creation simply with the plea that it is not his viewpoint but of his character. How can one disassociate himself with this plea? Aravind Adiga is the creator of the white tiger but is not himself the white tiger. He has created the tiger with the full freedom to eat anyone or anything that comes in its way in the name of self-examination. The white tiger and Adiga are different from each other and should be because of the philosophy: "Let animals live like animals; let humans live like humans" (276).

Adiga has honestly depicted true India with his imported western pen that moves smoothly on the roads of big cities in India and outside. To think that this pen will move on the roads of Bihar and UP is beyond imagination. But, it moves and writes fast. Now, come and enter the world of *The White Tiger* who is ready to welcome the Chinese Premier sharing the secret about India, that "One fact about India is that you can take almost anything you hear about the country from the prime minister and turn it upside down and then you will have the truth about that thing" (15). What the Indian Prime Minister says is not true. What he does not tell is true. It is India where the Prime Minister tells a lie and deceives the people by telling the things that are not. But, Adiga who is sincere and truthful, knows very well about the Indian Prime Minister. He dare not say what is not true. To think that it is Adiga who has said this will be an injustice to him because it is not he but the white tiger Balram Halwai who has made this statement. To consider what Balram Halwai says will be again injustice. That he is wrong is the reader's viewpoint. The white tiger thinks that what he says is right and it is his viewpoint.

Where has Adiga come in between? Again, Balram believes that his country is "the kind where it pays to play it both ways" and "the Indian entrepreneur has to be straight and crooked, mocking and believing, sly and sincere, at the same time" (19). Is it so? How can one be crooked and straight at the same time? But, for Balram, the Indian entrepreneur possesses this quality. It is surprising that why this tiger Balram is in Bangalore settled as an entrepreneur when he himself thinks that "There's no reward for entrepreneurship in most of India, Your Excellency. It's a sad fact" (59). Even then, he lives in India and does not settle down in America or any other country where he may get recognition. He loves China because of freedom-loving people. India is free but thinks that India has never been free. He moves further but has problem with the Indians who are now free but even then "don't understand the value of freedom" (117).

There is only one Indian who understands the value of freedom. That man is Balram Halwai. Even then he is living in India. He lives in India but loves China because he sees his future in or with China. Somewhere in his mind he thinks of becoming the boss with the help of China. Delhi is the capital of India but he knows the truth about Delhi. "The truth is that Delhi is a crazy city" (118) "where civilisation can appear and disappear within five minutes" (281). There is one driver with the diseased lip for whom the roads of Delhi are "good" but the people are "bad" (124). Are the people of Delhi really bad? Is it the driver's point of view, not of all? Adiga who knows the roads and the people of Delhi better will never make such statements. Then, who can make? Certainly, it is the character, not the creator of the character.

The unique quality that can be found only in Indians, not even in the English men is that "Everyone in India drinks and drives" (159). But, again, it is not Adiga who says it but his character Pinky Madam who has come from America only to see that every Indian drinks. Is she a teetotaller? She drinks and hits a boy. Adiga will certainly tell if interviewed on this point that all the Indians do not drink and all of them are not teetotallers. Do all the car-owners in Delhi have whisky in their cars? But, the Fat man is surprised and remarks: "Everyone has whisky in their car in Delhi, Ashok, didn't you know this" (213)? Who will tell the truth to the Fat man? This man also thinks that "Elections, my friend, can be managed in India. It's not like in America" (213). No doubt, India is not America but to think that elections are managed seems to be ridiculous. If it is so, there will be no need of the elections and the political parties.

The driver can drive well but not the car-owner because "no one follows any rules" (81). This is what Mr Ashok tells Pinky Madam. One needs a driver here. What does Ashok want to say? Is it confined only to the roads or to the country? Mr Ashok is rich and has the driver Balram but his beloved Uma thinks that "Delhi drivers are all rotten" and indulged in selling "drugs, and prostitutes, and God knows what else" (211). This is Uma's viewpoint, not of Ashok who cannot move without the driver. The other drivers tell Balram that "every rich man these days is divorcing his wife" (183). Is it so that every rich man is divorcing? What about poor people and their treatment with their wives? But, again, these are the drivers' viewpoint, not of all the men.

Now a question arises: who is right—whether Pinky Madam who thinks every Indian is a drunkard or Mr Ashok who thinks that Indians do not follow rules, or Balram Halwai who thinks that Indians including the Prime Minister tell lies and have double standards? Will Adiga clarify this confusion? But, again, these are different characters, each one thinking himself or herself right. Actually has not Adiga made an attack on India? How can he think so? Never, he is the well-wisher of India who with China is "likely to inherit the world from the west" (Wikipedia). What he is doing can be justified on the ground of "the greater process of self-examination" (Wikipedia). Adiga does not have any ill-will against India. How can he have any ill-will as he himself is an Indian? A doctor cannot be held responsible if he operates the patient. He has a sacred aim—the aim of caring for health and removing the pain, and for this if he has to operate, he does. Adiga is also a doctor, and a doctor in India, particularly in villages, becomes God-like. The doctor in Adiga, in the name of "the greater process of self-examination" (Wikipedia) has operated India on the Western table with the English knife. No doubt, the operation is successful and for this he is appreciated by the Western media which makes him forget the body of India that cries in pain to the extent that her genuine sons hear her cries even outside. He feels the pain of India in his heart but the West has taught him only how to operate, not how to cure. His condition is just like Balram who himself does not know what he has done. He fails to connect the things which confuse him like the wires in the bonnet of a car.

> Remember, Mr Premier, the first time, perhaps as a boy, when you opened the bonnet of a car and looked into its entrails? Remember the coloured wires twisting from one part of the engine to the other, the black box full of yellow caps, enigmatic tubes hissing out steam and oil and grease everywhere—remember how mysterious and magical everything seemed? When I peer into the portion of my story that unfolds in New Delhi, I feel the same way. If you ask me to explain how one event connects to another, or how one motive strengthens or weakens the next, or how I went from thinking *this* about my master to thinking *that*—I will tell you that I myself don't understand these things. I cannot be certain that the story, as I will tell it, is the right story to tell. (113)

Adiga has created the characters that are now not in his hands as they have their individuality and identity with the illusions that they are right while others are wrong. God becomes unseen after creating people; the creator also becomes detached if not unseen after creating his characters. But, again the question strikes: what is the fault of these characters that are the product of one mind? The mind is of the creator who is one, not many, then, how can he disassociate himself with his characters?

The white tiger is white not because of his colour but because of his longing for power and pelf. If it had not been white, it would have dyed to make itself white. Is the white tiger afraid of the lizard? No. But, the tiger Balram is afraid of the lizard. The thing that keeps the lizard away and makes him feel in the light is the chandelier. Balram keeps the chandelier everywhere to make himself aware of the light and also to forget darkness—the darkness of the village that he has already left behind and the memories in the form of family members, of whom he has performed the last rites so that he may live in peace. What he does more is that he has changed his name in order to forget the painful memories related with the name of Balram.

Balram is a servant on the verge of a slave while Ashok Sharma is the master without the qualities of being master. The master lacks "balls" and the tiger in Balram comes to know about this fact. Then, he makes up his mind to sacrifice this lamb to be the master of the jungle. He murders him, steals his red bag containing seven hundred thousand rupees and becomes the master of drivers in Bangalore. Though he talks of freeing the poor people from slavery with a revolution, he wears the dress of his master Ashok Kumar. He is not satisfied even with this as he changes his name and becomes himself Ashok Sharma, the white tiger. Why does the tiger use the name of the lamb? He mocks at the upper caste strata but even then loves to eat and enjoy life like them. Why does Balram Halwai use 'Sharma', a tag of the upper caste with the changed name 'Ashok' in spite of being a champion of the *dalits* and the exploited, the subaltern section? The reader does not know. One man knows the answer and he is the creator of this character but he has dissociated himself from his characters who are left to live their own life in the jungle. But, one thing is certain, this tiger loves the red colour—whether it is the colour of sex, particularly a virgin of seventeen or eighteen years, or of red petticoat of Nepali women or the bag that contained seven hundred thousand rupees.

What the school inspector thought has been proved by Balram Halwai who differentiated himself initially from the students and later from the people by becoming the white tiger, "the rarest of animals—the creature that comes along only once in a generation" (35). This white tiger will sell everything and with the money; he will start "a school—an English language school—for poor children in Bangalore" (320) where "the facts of life" will be taught, not the stories of Gandhi or God. The poor students will become the white tigers whom Balram Halwai will let loose in Bangalore in order to have the city in control. Then, he will make the assistant commissioner of police sit "on a bicycle and have Asif knock him over it with the Qualis" (320).

Somewhere, the tiger dreams of a utopia, which is on the verge of communism. He dreams the dream though he knows it will "turn out to be nothing" (320). The tiger dreams the dreams which helped him in breaking the rooster coop of the family, of slavery, of circumstances and of secularism in the past, he hopes so in future also. Dreams are essential if one wishes to see beautiful. He knows: *"They remain slaves because they can't see what is beautiful in this world"* (40). The man looks for "the key" (253) but does not dream. Hence, the need is of dreaming dreams that make a man see the door open.

The white tiger becomes poetic when he recites the lines: *"You were looking for the key for years / But the door was always open"* (253)! The tiger dreams with open eyes, not with closed ones. He mentions a story of Buddha and a cunning Brahmin. The cunning Brahmin who intends to trick the Buddha asks him: "Master, do you consider yourself a man or a god?" and gets the response from the Buddha who smiles and says: "Neither. I am just one who has woken up while the rest of you are still sleeping" (315). If Mr Jiabao asks Balram whether he is a man or demon, his response will also be like that of the Buddha. He is neither a man nor a demon. How can he be a man or a god as he is the tiger, an animal with brain though he claims that he has woken up while the rest are still sleeping? Yes, the tiger is waking while the other animals are sleeping. He knows that if other animals wake up, they will force him to run away from the jungle.

Adiga has not followed his character Balram Halwai and so he does the pious job of awakening the people of India. He rings the bell of self-examination which makes them rise up. The waking West sees the sleeping East and laughs calling it 'Other'. Adiga uses palliative to alleviate pain without curing with the intention that Indians will cure themselves with the Western medicines though he himself suggests to the West how to cure the mental stress with the Eastern yoga. The Eastern yoga is the panacea that keeps the white tiger away from the stresses, otherwise he would go mad. The tiger does not accept it before the East but shares the Indian secret with the Chinese Premier with the suggestion to make "yoga a must in all Chinese schools" (292) and also an invitation from his side for joining "in the killing". The tiger states: "The future of a real estate is Bangalore, Mr Jiabao. You can join in the killing if you want—I'll help you out" (319)!

To the white tiger Balram Halwai, a Nepali known for his faithfulness, becomes faithless to his master, and the Muslims whom he meets are illiterate looking for "buildings to blow up"(40) and their language Urdu which is "all just scratches and dots, as if some crow dipped its feet in black ink and pressed them to the page" (253). For him, the Hindus' gods are not gods but the "divine arses" who, like our politicians "seem to do awfully little work" and "yet keep winning re-election to their golden thrones in heaven, year after year" (8). He mocks at all the religions except Buddhism because of the fear of China where he sees his future. Mark the excerpt for the meaning of Dharma (religion) which the tiger, in spite of knowing the fact, does not accept its presence because of his communistic soul that erases the word 'dharma' from the dictionary:

> 'What's your name, boy?'
>
> 'Dharam.'
>
> 'What a nice name. Do you know what it means?'
>
> 'Yes, sir.'
>
> 'Does your uncle know what it means?'
>
> 'Shut up,' I said. (265)

This is a conversation between Dharam and Vitiligo-Lips. The uncle is Balram Halwai who closes the discussion because he does not expect anyone to talk over *Dharam*. How can one expect this tiger to be religious when he himself keeps Dharam under his thumb? He breaks the myth of his caste 'Halwai' by becoming a driver and later on an entrepreneur.

The man from the Darkness can enter the area of Lightness and has the potential of producing the light for others. A halwai does not drink but he breaks the myth and begins to drink. For him, women are not women but commodities for sale. He removes the sticker of Kali because it looks like his granny Kusum. Everything is "rotten" here. He sees wrong in everything, be it politics, religion, economy, education, judiciary or any other thing, and even then the tiger lives in Bangalore, the city of Lightness, not in Mumbai where "everyone goes in the films" (297) after killing someone.

Balram has not murdered the Lamb Mr Ashok. Rather, he has performed the pious act of redemption through shedding the blood. The sacrifice to become a man cannot be a murder. One sacrifice is sufficient to be a man and also to come out from the coop of slavery.

The creator of Balram Halwai is not like his character. He is frank and candid in mocking and butchering India for her good with a pious act of self-examination for her health. Is this a murder? No, it cannot be. If it had been the case, the creator would have never settled in Mumbai. The creator knows English well and makes even characters from the village speak in English. It is a great achievement when Balram uses polished words like 'beak' for penis and 'arse' for 'anus'. He does not abuse in Hindi but in Pinky Madam's favourite phrase:

"What a fucking joke!" The dirty becomes posh from his magical pen.

The tiger knows that this age is of consumerism where the black wears the white dress and the white black because of their saleability. Even the cover of the novel is symbolic and speaks the language of the white tiger. The word 'WHITE' is properly written with the point above the letter 'I' while the 'TIGER' has the point below the letter. Is it not the miracle of the brain? The white is the West, full of power—power of putting things in their own way while the tiger is Indian. *The White Tiger* dishes out the Indian matter with the Western ceremony. Whether the tiger is the real one or not creates doubts in the mind. The white tiger is initially a driver and a driver cannot see "the whole picture" (140). What he sees are "just flashes, glimpses, bits of conversation", so then how can he claim to present a true image of India? Besides this, he is "not an original thinker" but "an original *listener*" (47) who presents the incomplete picture of India, but the picture is liked by the Western Pinky Madam who calls him "a fucking genius" (160) and gives him "a brown envelope" (181) containing money. A great creation from a genius! How well the creator has butchered India on the Western slab in the name of greater process of self-examination! Really, he deserves something different, even greater than the Booker Prize.

Works Cited

Adiga, Aravind. *The White Tiger*. New Delhi: HarperCollins, 2008. **Print.**

http://en.wikipedia.org/wiki/Aravind_Adiga. Web.

2

Divine Arses

Vulgar words that abuse Hindus' gods vehemently, the colours that paint India's derogatory picture highlighting her poverty, bribery and corruption so that it may please the Western eyes that wish to see her on the periphery as 'Other', the rational philosophy that may rationalise that the causes of India's backwardness are her family and democratic system, etc., are some of the ingredients that make the recipe for bagging any prize, particularly the Booker. The Booker Prize Committee found Aravind Adiga the most suitable young Indian novelist because of his twenty-four carat gold-like purity in the substance of self-denigration, i.e., Indian life. Is this self-denigration a planned way of getting favour from China, the ideal country for him? Is the White Tiger a really thinking man who is writing the tips of entrepreneurship for the Chinese Premier? Is he not laying out the dark side of Indian culture on the Western table only to display that India's spirituality is fake. Is he a cruel Marxist who feels proud of himself in defaming the Indian heritage? The best has become the worst from his pen. What has he got from the people of India? But, certainly, the West has taken him in its lap and given a lollipop of a Booker Prize.

Aravind Adiga's *The White Tiger* is narrated in the form of a long series of unanswered letters (epistolatory technique) from the desk of Ashok Sharma, the white tiger of Bangalore, erstwhile Balram Halwai. Through the letters addressed to His Excellency, Wen Jiabao, the Premier's Office, Beijing, the capital of the freedom-loving nation of China, Balram confesses the truth of his entrepreneurship. The narration unfolds not only the life-story of Balram but also the corrupt system that works in two Indias—India of Light and India of Darkness. Munna becomes Balram because of his naming by the teacher Krishna. As the school inspector finds him a promising young boy, he not only calls him the white tiger but also promises him that he will recommend his name to the authorities for scholarship. But, unfortunately, because of the family loan, he has to leave the school to work at tea-shop as a bonded labourer. But, this white tiger continues to learn through eavesdropping. As he is different, he learns driving and finally becomes a chauffeur to the Stork family. Cunningly he removes the two hurdles, i.e., the Nepali guard and the old driver Ram Persad, and comes to Delhi with Mr Ashok and Pinky Madam. As he is not born to be a servant forever, he wishes to do something different. He murders Ashok, takes his red bag containing seven hundred thousand rupees, runs with Dharam and finally comes to Bangalore where he settles down with the help of the police whom he bribes, and becomes an entrepreneur. This is the life-story of Balram Halwai shot in the gripping and entertaining mode with the window camera that views the surface as it has no power to peep into the depth. Throughout the story that he narrates in the letters addressed to the Chinese Premier, he seems to be mocking at the religions, particularly the Hindu religion.

Before going into the details of the mockery of religions which Adiga does through his protagonist Balram Halwai, it is mandatory to know what religion is and what role it plays in shaping the Indian culture. Religion, which is a psychic urge with thought, will and feeling, actually embraces the faith that conserves values which help a man in realising God. It is a force that unifies all in one thread. India is India because of spirituality. This spirituality is the outcome of the long process of worship and devotion of the rishis and munis who guided the people to a disciplined and religious life, hence contributed in stabilising the society. Jawaharlal Nehru realises the importance of religion recommending that it should face life with "the temper and approach of science, allied to philosophy, and with reverence for all that lies beyond" (*The Discovery of India* 527) to avoid checking "the tendency to change and progress inherent in human society" (*The Discovery of India* 524). India does not need to give up its religions because if she does, disaster will occur. Nikhilandanda states: "If India gives up religion and takes exclusively to politics, science, and technology to build her future, she will be courting disaster. All of her national activities must be inspired by religion. This seems to be mandate of India's past" (*Hinduism* 14-15). Emphasizing the relationship, he, further, writes: "The separation of science and religion has been a major tragedy for the human race. The relationship between them may be linked to that of body and soul; the body without a soul is a mere corpse, and the soul without a body, a mere phantom" (*Hinduism* 15).

In order to be in the good books of the West for material gains in the form of awards and rewards, writers denounce India and her religious aura. To the contrary, there are some foreigners like Max Muller who do not hesitate in praising India for her spirituality. Aravind Adiga must learn from Max Muller who realised the true strength of India in illumining the inner life. Material gains are immaterial as they can provide the pleasure of body, not of soul. Max Muller writes: "If one would ask me under what sky the human mind has most fully developed its precious gifts, has scrutinised most profoundly the greatest problems of life, and has, at least for some, provided solutions which deserve to be admired even by those who have studied Plato and Kant, I would indicate India. And if one would ask me which literature would give us back (us Europeans, who have been exclusively fed on Greek and Roman thought, and on that of a Semitic race) the necessary equilibrium in order to make our inner life more perfect, more comprehensive, more universal, in short, more human, a life not only for this life, but for a transformed and eternal life, once again I would indicate India" (qtd. *Hinduism* 20). Adiga should study the history of India to know that whenever "the country was spiritually great it was also materially prosperous and culturally creative" (*Hinduism* 14).

It seems that Adiga is more interested in mocking at the name of Rama, the ideal man, than any other name. That's why he names his characters with the word Ram either in the beginning as Ram Dev (Stork) Ram Pandey (the Doctor), Ramanathan (a fixer) and Ram Bahadur (Nepali Guard) or in the end as Balram (the Protagonist) or Vikram (Father of Balram). None of them possesses the qualities of Ram.

In the novel, the protagonist Balram considers himself Hanuman serving his Rama (Mr Ashok) and Sita (Pinky Madam). Later, this Hanuman kills his own master Rama. When he consoles his master Mr Ashok who has lost charms when Pinky Madam leaves him, he thinks himself to be Krishna, a charioteer who counselled Arjuna in the battlefield.

Later, he realises that he should cut the Mongoose's neck. The Mongoose is Mukesh. Mukesh is the other name of Shiva, who killed Muka, a demon in the form of a wild boar. He himself admits that the name of Shiva is truth.

In Bangalore, Balram becomes Ashok. The meaning of Ashok is 'without sorrow'. This name is also associated with Ashok, a third century BC emperor of India. Seeing the massacre at Kalinga, the violent Ashoka became non-violent and embraced Buddhism.

But, after killing his master Mr Ashok and stealing his red bag full of money, Balram settles down assuming the name of Mr Ashok Sharma. But, this Ashok Sharma does not follow any religion, rather keeps Dharam with him and intends to kill him if he thinks of the family in the village. Dharam means religion. Balram, who has become the boss of Bangalore, has kept Dharam, i.e., religion under his thumb. He feels pleasure either in giving pains to the names beginning with Ram or seeing them being pained by others.

The Stork whose real name is Ram Dev bows down before the Great Socialist. Dr. Ram Pandey gives a part of his salary to the politician to continue his private practice without going to the government hospital. He makes Ram Bahadur, the Nepali guard, silent and bow down before him. Ram Persad is not Ram Persad but Mohammad who has taken the garb of Ram Persad only to get the job in a Hindu family. All these names beginning with Ram or ending with Ram are named not by chance but are preplanned by Aravind Adiga with the intention of mocking at the religion, particularly Hindu religion.

Adiga is quite allergic to calling India saintly and moral. His protagonist Balram Halwai though declares that he does not know how to speak English like the Chinese Premier, he can say certain things in English because of their false aroma. He is not against great men but when he sees the Indian Prime Minister and his cronies telling about Indian spirituality, he feels uncomfortable. He writes to the Chinese premier: "But whenever I see our prime minister and his distinguished sidekicks drive to the airport in black cars and get out and do *namastes* before you in front of a TV camera and tell you about how moral and saintly India is, I have to say that thing in English" (*The White Tiger* 4). Writing this in the letter, he asks him not to believe in what the Indian Prime Minister says about India where "the Indian entrepreneur has to be straight and crooked, mocking and believing, sly and sincere, at the same time" (*The White Tiger* 9). Such a sweeping statement seems to be absurd and highly prejudiced. For him, all the Indian entrepreneurs are hypocrites who cannot remain the same at one time. What 786 is for Muslims, the image of the *ishta devi or devta* is for Hindus. Whether it is the movie or anything, Hindu likes to see "the picture of a woman in white sari with gold sovereigns dripping down to her feet, which is the goddess Lakshmi" (*The White Tiger* 8). It is a part of Indian culture to begin any work with a prayer. Mark the derogatory words that Adiga makes Balram speak:

> I guess, Your Excellency, that I too should start off by kissing some god's arse.
>
> Which god's arse, though? There are so many choices.
>
> See, the Muslims have one god.

> The Christians have three gods.
>
> And we Hindus have 36,000,000 gods.
>
> Making a grant total of 36,000,004 divine arses for me to choose from.
>
> (*The White Tiger* 8)

To call gods 'arses' is indeed an insult to India and her culture. Arse, according to Wordweb, is the fleshy part of the human body that one sits on. It is a vulgar slang for anus. Adiga may be an atheist or a staunch believer in the principles of communism but he has no right to call gods 'arses'. If the excerpt is minutely studied, he includes even Christianity and Islam and later Buddhism. For him, there are 36,000,000 Hindu gods, one Muslim god and three Christian gods making a total of 36,000,004 divine arses, among which he has to choose one. Later, he adds one more name to the list—Buddha—when he answers the question of the inspector about Buddha saying first that he was 'An enlightened man', then, 'An enlightened *god*.' What Adiga writes in bracket is worth-noting (Oops! Thirty-six million and five—!) (*The White Tiger* 34). He adds one more name—Buddha—to the list that now has total of thirty-six million and five. But, what is worthnoting is the hyphen after the word five. Is he afraid of the Chinese Premier or China where the followers of Buddhism reside? Has he no courage to fill the gap with the word 'arses'. Very cunningly he abuses as well as shows his respect for them.

There are some thinking men who think that these gods do not exist. He declares that he is not a philosopher and, hence, does not know the truth but somehow he feels that there is "just us and an ocean of darkness around us" (*The White Tiger* 8). Here he seems to be a follower of Marx who does not believe in religion which is simply opium for him. He compares these gods to the politicians who have no work except winning re-election. He hurts the religious feelings of the Hindus in spite of his claim of not disrespecting them. Mark the excerpt:

> Now, there are some, and I don't mean Communists like you, but thinking men of all political parties, who think that not many of these gods actually exist. Some believe that *none* of them exist. There's just us and an ocean of darkness around us. I'm no philosopher or poet, how would I know the truth? It's true that all these gods seem to do awfully little work—much like our politicians—and yet keep winning re-election to their golden thrones in heaven, year after year. That's not to say that I don't respect them, Mr Premier! Don't you ever let that blasphemous idea into your yellow skull. (*The White Tiger* 8)

Balram closes his eyes, folds his hands in "a reverent Namaste" and prays to the gods for inspiration. He asks Mr Jiabao to bear with him as it will take a few minutes to recall gods in his memory. He opens his eyes and makes a very irreligious statement, "How quickly do you think you could kiss 36,000,004 arses" (*The White Tiger* 9)? To use words *'kiss'* and *'arses'* again is too much. What is he trying to offer before the world? Do Indians think about gods in terms of 'kiss' and 'arses'? He is foul-mouthed and blasphemous. He has mocked at the polytheism but he does not know that this polytheism ultimately results in monotheism. Swami Nikhilananda writes in this connection:

> The deities of popular Hinduism are symbols of the Personal God. Their images are seen in the temples and shrines. A popular saying in India speaks of three hundred million and thirty-three thousand deities worshipped by three hundred million people. Yet the Hindu religion is essentially monotheistic. Whatever deity or aspect of reality is worshipped is, to his devotee, the supreme God, other deities being only parts of Him. Therefore the monotheism of the Hindus does not exclude other gods; it includes them all. (*Hinduism* 162)

Though outwardly the Hindu religion is polytheism, it is actually monotheism in spirit. Here, prayer is the medium to share and commune with the personal deity who is part of the Supreme power, i.e., God. A man worships a deity "either for the fulfillment of worldly desires or for ultimate deliverance from the bondage of the world" (*Hinduism* 163). The protagonist of *The White Tiger* is a curious mixture because of his indecisive nature. Sometimes he seems to be a theist, sometimes an atheist, and sometimes to be oscillating between the two. The Black Fort near Laxmangarh always attracts him but he fails to reach there. Finally he succeeds in stepping into the Fort and goes to the highest point from where he sees the temple tower, the market, the sewage, the landlord's mansion and his own house. All these things look beautiful but there he does something too disgusting to describe. Mark his words:

> My little Laxmangarh. I saw the temple tower, the market, the glistening line of sewage, the landlords' mansions—and my own house, with that dark little cloud outside—the water buffalo. It looked like the most beautiful sight on earth.
>
> I leaned out from the edge of the fort in the direction of my village—and then I did something too disgusting to describe you.
>
> Well, actually, I spat. Again and again. And then, whistling and humming, I went back down the hill.
>
> Eight months later, I slit Mr Ashok's throat.
>
> (*The White Tiger* 42)

His spitting again and again reflects his hatred for the traditions which he determines to give up for the sake of the change that he wishes to bring into his life. It results in the murder of Mr Ashok whose red bag full of money he takes and runs finally to settle down in Bangalore where he becomes a white tiger. Later, when he remembers Iqbal's devil who expresses his dissents at God's command of becoming a servant, he thinks of "a little black figure in a wet khaki uniform who is climbing up the entranceway to a black fort" (*The White Tiger* 87). He puts himself in place of the devil before God who asks him: "*Isn't it all wonderful? Isn't it all grand? Aren't you grateful to be my servant*?" In response to this question, the boy in wet khaki uniform starts shaking with "anger, before delivering to the Almighty a gesture of thanks for having created the world this particular way, instead of all the other ways it could have been created" (*The White Tiger* 88). While sitting under the chandelier, Balram Halwai sees "the little man in the khaki uniform *spitting* at God again and again" (*The White Tiger* 88).

Adiga ridicules the Hindu religion indicating a power structure—a kind of hierarchy among Hindu gods. He never sees the unity or oneness but searches for the way of division. He divides India into two—India of Darkness and India of Light with the parameter of river and ocean. The people living in the area of Darkness worship the deities of the lower order while the people living in the area of Light worship the deity of super structures for power. Hanuman belongs to the lower category because of his being a servant to Lord Rama. Hence, Hanuman is a popular deity among the people living in the Darkness. Mark the excerpt which Adiga makes Balram say to the Chinese Premier:

> Inside, you will find an image of a saffron-coloured creature, half man half monkey: this is Hanuman, everyone's favourite god in the Darkness. Do you know about Hanuman, sir? He was the faithful servant of the god Rama, and we worship him in our temples because he is a shining example of how to serve your masters with absolute fidelity, love, and devotion.
>
> These are the kinds of gods they have foisted on us, Mr Jiabao. Understand, now, how hard it is for a man to win his freedom in India. (*The White Tiger* 19)

Balram Halwai considers religion as the cause of Indian slavery as it never allows the people to rise against the master. For him, man cannot be free in India only because of the system, the cage that has imprisoned the people who feel happy while living there to their satisfaction. He sees politics even in the worship of the deities of the lower order so that people of the Darkness may remain servants like Hanuman to their master Rama with all devotion and fidelity. Will anyone convince Adiga's Halwai that worship is a personal affair and one can choose one's deity according to one's wish without any coercion?

Adiga's Balram Halwai uses religion in getting job. He tries to show that he is the right person, who never steals, never disrespects God and who never utters blasphemies. Mark the excerpt for Halwai's falsehood for the sake of getting the job of a chauffeur:

> I swear by God, sir—I swear by all 36,000,004 of them—the moment I saw his face, I knew: *This is the master for me.*
>
> I just had to divert this Nepali fucker as long as possible.
>
> 'I'm a good driver, sir. I don't smoke, I don't drink, I don't steal.'
>
> 'Fuck off, don't you understand?'
>
> 'I don't disrespect my God, I don't disrespect my family.'
>
> 'What's wrong with you? Get lost, at once—'
>
> 'I don't gossip about my masters, I don't steal, I don't blaspheme.'
>
> (*The White Tiger* 60)

He speaks this to divert the Nepali guard Ram Bahadur and to attract the attention of the master so that he may listen to him and offer the job. All these promises are forgotten as soon as he gets the job. Telling a lie for getting a job is permissible and acceptable in his dictionary. Adiga's politics of mocking does not stop here. He lashes at the Hindu religion through the description of the cars—Maruti and Honda. Mark the description:

> Now, there were two cars in the garage. One was your standard Maruti Suzuki—that little white car you see all over India—the other was the Honda City. Now, the Maruti is a small, simple fellow, a perfect servant to the driver; the moment you turn the ignition key, he does exactly what the driver wants him to. The Honda City is a larger car, a more sophisticated creature, with a mind of his own; he has power steering, and an advanced engine, and he does what *he* wants to. (*The White Tiger* 62)

The word 'Maruti', the other name of Hanuman, is used in a derogatory sense. Everyone knows that cars are used and called in feminine gender. Here Adiga has used Maruti in the masculine form knowingly to make fun of Hanuman, the deity worshipped and respected by everyone, irrespective of his status. Here, Maruti becomes a car of "your standard Maruti Suzuki". Why has he used the word 'your' before standard? Does he wish to show that the premier's standard is only of having a car like Maruti Suzuki or is there any other way round? Again the phrase "that little white car you see all over India" makes his intention clear. Is he not again indicating the people of India through the Maruti, on whom he can have control and use them like servants in future? Honda is a car in which China has invested money. He always uses Honda, a car with its own mind, while Maruti is a perfect car for being a servant to the driver. Who is the driver? Is he not indicating the Chinese Premier as a future driver?

Both the drivers, Ram Persad and Balram Halwai, live together. Ram Persad, who begins his day with the prayer chanting 'Om' and bowing "in front of at least twenty pictures of various gods" (*The White Tiger* 77), looks at Balram with a gesture of inquiry: "*Don't you pray? What are you, a Naxal* (*The White Tiger* 77)? He feels insulted, goes to the market, buys "two dozen of the cheapest idols of Hanuman and Ram" (*The White Tiger* 78) and places them in his room. His action is a reaction to Ram Persad with whom he may compete now. His statement "So both of us now had the same number of gods in the room; and we drowned out each other's prayers in the morning while bowing before our respective deities" (*The White Tiger* 78) clearly reflects his own satisfaction. It is only a way of mocking at religion. Outwardly both Ram Persad and Balram Halwai are Hindus but in reality a Muslim is making fun of Balram, a Hindu, that he is a naxal, an atheist. His case reminds the reader of Aziz disguised as Vishnu Prasad in Girish Karnad's *Tughlaq*. Here, Mohammad is disguised as Ram Persad. Was the disguise of a Hindu necessary for getting a job? Only Adiga can answer this. Was there not any other option left for Mohammad? To show a Muslim bowing and praying before the deities seems strange. At least, he does not intend to show the bond of Hindus and Muslims. If he wishes to, there is no need of disguise.

The manner by which Halwai tries to expose Ram Persad is also not proper though later he feels guilty. Ambition subsides his feeling. Ram Persad goes leaving "all his images of gods behind", which he puts into a bag. For him, those things (images of gods) are handy as they can be put in a bag.

The protagonist Balram Halwai also points out the strange belief of the Muslims who feel that the number 786 will do miracles in life as it evokes a religious feeling for God. "Just before the movie got started, the number 786 would flash against the black screen—the Muslims think this is a magic number that represents their God" (8). He is also surprised that all the four great poets of the world are Muslims in spite of the lower literary ratio among them. He appreciates Iqbal for speaking the truth about slaves but the way he appreciates shows his mental attitude which is certainly anti-Muslim. Mark the excerpt:

> Iqbal, who is one of the four best poets in the world—the others being Rumi, Mirza Ghalib, and a fourth fellow, also a Muslim, whose name I've forgotten—has written a poem where he says this about slaves:
>
> *They remain slaves because they can't see what is beautiful in this world.*
>
> That's the truest thing anyone ever said.
>
> A great poet, this fellow Iqbal—even if he *was* a Muslim.
>
> (By the way, Mr Premier: have you noticed that all four of the greatest poets in the world are Muslim? And yet all the Muslims you meet are illiterate or covered head to toe in black burkas or looking for buildings to blow up? It's a puzzle, isn't it? If you ever figure these people out, send me an e-mail.) (*The White Tiger* 40)

What Adiga makes Balram Halwai speak within brackets is shameful and needs no comments. Sample one more excerpt:

> Mr Ashok joined the game. He stood as the wicketkeeper while I bowled full tosses to the brat.
>
> 'I'm Azharuddin, captain of India!' the boy shouted every time he hit a six or a four.

> 'Call yourself Gavaskar. Azharuddin is a Muslim.'
>
> It was the Stork. He had come into the courtyard to watch.
>
> Mr Ashok said, 'Father, what a silly thing to say! Hindu or Muslim, what difference does it make?'
>
> (*The White Tiger* 70)

Here again, the anti-Muslim attitude of the Stork who does not wish that his grandson should call himself by a Muslim name like Azharuddin is obvious. No doubt, people like the Stork suffering from narrow-mindedness are in India. If the people like the Stork are present, people like Ashok who oppose this mean mentality come to the front and create harmony through their humanistic attitude—that all human beings are equal and are children of the same god.

Balram is a hypocrite in the sense that on the one hand he mocks at the gods while on the other hand he attempts to pray for their blessings. When he takes out Honda City for the first time, he prays to the gods lest he should commit a mistake as he is not used to driving it. He states: "I still wasn't used to the Honda City, which is a moody car with a mind of its own, as I've said. I just prayed to the gods—all of them—not to let me make a mistake" (*The White Tiger* 80). He knows that the Honda City is a moody car over which he has no control. While driving with Pinky Madam and Ashok sitting in the back seat, he considers himself to be Hanuman who is carrying Ram and Sita on his shoulder. He thinks of himself as faithful as Hanuman who is devoted wholeheartedly to Lord Rama and Sita. Mark the devotion that the excerpt reveals:

> Now another face appears, to the side of his, in memory's mirror. Pinky Madam—his wife. Every bit as good-looking as her husband; just as the image of the goddess in the Birla Hindu Temple in New Delhi is as fair as the god to whom she is married. She would sit in the back, and the two of them would talk, and I would drive them wherever they wanted, as faithfully as the servant-god Hanuman carried about his master and mistress, Ram and Sita. (*The White Tiger* 46)

Later this devoted servant Hanuman changes the equation, acts like Ravana and kills his master Ashok Kumar.

While driving in her drunkard state, Pinky Madam hits a boy. Balram signs the affidavit and takes the responsibility of the accident. He himself does not know what to do and the idea of running away from there never enters his mind. Servants have to take the responsibility of the crimes which are committed by their masters. When the case of hit-and-run is not reported, there is no need of going to jail. He goes to "a nearby Hanuman temple to say a prayer of thanks" (*The White Tiger* 181). It is surprising that in spite of having no devotion at all, he goes to the temple where he prays. It seems that inwardly he is afraid of the power of gods but outwardly does not accept them and mocks while narrating the story to the Chinese Premier. He also goes to the temple to pray for Mr Ashok and Pinky Madam for their long, happy married life. Somehow he feels insecure that if the marriage breaks, the master will return to the village and again he will have no job. The fear of losing his job takes him to the temple where he prays for his master and mistress. "The next day I went to a roadside temple in Gurgaon. I put a rupee before the two resident pairs of divine arses and prayed that Pinky Madam and Mr Ashok should be reunited and given a long and happy life together in Delhi" (*The White Tiger* 187).

Swami Nikhilananda states: "The physical symbols used in the popular religion of modern India are classified into two groups; either they may be natural objects such as a tree, the sun, a river, fire, or a special piece of stone, or they may be images or pictures. These symbols remind the devotees of certain aspects, powers, and attributes of the Godhead" (*Hinduism* 167). While returning from the village, Balram Halwai knowingly tries to demonstrate his religiousness by bowing his head before a tree. At a query from Ashok, he tells that he has shown respect to the sacred tree. Both Ashok and Pinky Madam are convinced at the religious nature of Balram Halwai who does it knowingly to win their favour. Generally it is believed that a man of religious nature never deceives his master. Mark the conversation:

> 'The villagers are so religious in the Darkness.'
>
> That seemed to have impressed the two of them, so I put my finger to my eye a moment later, again.
>
> 'What's that for, driver? I don't see any temples around.'
>
> 'Er... we drove past a sacred tree, sir. I was offering my respects.'
>
> 'Did you hear that? They worship nature. It's beautiful, isn't it?'
>
> They were convinced I was the most religious servant on earth. (Take *that*, Ram Persad!)
>
> (*The White Tiger* 90-91)

Somewhere in the mind of Balram Halwai was Ram Persad whose religious nature was unquestioned. Before Ashok and Pinky Madam, he succeeds in proving himself to be the most religious servant on earth. Does it not sound strange that man takes the help of religion to deceive while the very spirit of religion is against any kind of deception?

Hindus worship female deities like Kali, Durga etc. as they "represent the Sakti, or creative power, of Brahman. Brahman and its power are inseparable" (*Hinduism* 168). These deities represent various powers of the spirit. Aravind Adiga makes his protagonist have the stickers and statues of goddess Lakshmi and Kali representing wealth and strength respectively in the car. But, the way he has depicted is not decent. It is purely taunting as it only ridicules the Hindu's belief in having them in their vehicles. Mark the description:

> The car had to be wiped with a soft, wet cloth, inside and outside; a stick of incense had to be placed at the small statue of the goddess Lakshmi, goddess of wealth, which sat above the dashboard—this had the double advantage of getting rid of the mosquitoes that had sneaked in at night, and scenting the insides with an aroma of religion. I wiped the seats—nice, plush leather seats; I wiped the dials; I lifted the leather mats on the floor and slapped the dust out of them. There were three magnetic stickers with images of the mother-goddess Kali on the

> dashboard—I had put them there, throwing out Ram Persad's magnetic stickers; I wiped them all. (*The White Tiger* 132)

Balram Halwai wipes the car and places a stick of incense before the statue of goddess Lakshmi. This will create a religious atmosphere in the car and also provide him a means to get rid of the mosquito. It seems that he is more afraid of the mosquito than the goddess of wealth "which sat above the dashboard". To use the word "which" is an insult to Lakshmi who is not a female goddess, rather a neuter or a dead thing for him. He brings the magnetic stickers with the images of Kali and places them in the car. He throws out Ram Persad's stickers and this action again shows Balram Halwai's anti-Muslim attitude. He throws them because they were brought by a Muslim. The stickers with Kali's images do not count for him. What counts for Halwai is a Muslim in the disguise of Ram Persad for whom he (Halwai) shows his hatred by throwing out his magnetic stickers. A religious man, irrespective of caste, colour or creed, expresses his love and devotion to the images of Kali.

Balram knows that he will not be allowed to enter the mall because of his poverty. He wears a white T-shirt, punches the ogre three times and touches "the stickers of the goddess Kali, with her long red tongue, for good luck" (*The White Tiger* 151). Adiga ridicules at the mentality of the Hindus. He makes his protagonist act in a very sacrilegious manner. Halwai punches the ogre now a dozen times, looks at "the magnetic stickers of goddess Kali with her skulls and her long red tongue" (*The White Tiger* 156), sticks his "tongue out at the old witch" and then yawns. To use the word 'old witch' for the goddess Kali again is a blasphemous act committed by Adiga through Balram Halwai. Then, again, this Halwai touches the sticker wishing for luck, not for a good action but for success in the murder of his master Ashok. He states: "I touched the magnetic stickers of the goddess Kali for luck, then opened the glove compartment. There it was—the broken bottle, with its claws of glass" (*The White Tiger* 281). When he murders his master, he pulls out all the stickers and throws them on the dead body of Ashok so that he may reach heaven. "I pulled out all the stickers of the goddess, and threw them on Mr Ashok's body—just in case they'd help his soul go to heaven" (*The White Tiger* 286). Again, the use of the words like "pulled out", "threw" "in case they'd" reflect the intensity of his hatred for the Hindu religion. Adiga, who is a Marxist in disguise, makes Balram Halwai his mouthpiece to reveal his hatred for religion. Halwai, a *rakshasha* in the disguise of Hanuman-like servant kills his Ram-like master without feeling any shame just for the sake of the red bag full of money. His throwing of the stickers reflects his throwing of his religion.

Balram Halwai, who mocks at the Hindu religion, makes his master Ashok laugh when he finds him in a depressed mood because of Pinky Madam's leaving him forever. Mark the excerpt for the mockery of religion:

> 'Sometimes I wonder, Balram. I wonder what's the point of living. I really wonder...'
>
> *The point of living? My heart pounded. The point of your living is that if you die, who's going to pay me three and a half thousand rupees a month?*
>
> 'You must believe in God, sir. You must go on. My granny says that if you believe in God, then good things will happen.'
>
> 'That's true, it's true. We must believe,' he sobbed.
>
> 'Once there was a man who stopped believing in God, and you know what happened?'
>
> 'What?'
>
> 'His buffalo died at once.'
>
> 'I see.' he laughed. 'I see.'
>
> 'Yes, sir, it really happened. The next day he said. "God, I'm sorry, I believe in You," and guess what happened?'
>
> 'His buffalo came back to life?"
>
> 'Exactly!'
>
> He laughed again. I told him another story, and this made him laugh some more.
>
> (*The White Tiger* 186)

For the fear of losing his job and salary of three thousand and five hundred rupees, Balram attempts to make him laugh in order to create his interest in life. He does it at the cost of mocking at the Hindu religion. Stopping the belief in God can make the buffalo die while belief in God can bring back it to life. He thinks himself to be Krishna who advises Arjuna to be ready to fight against the Kauravas. He attempts to make Mr. Ashok ready to fight in the battle because of the fear of losing his job. Mark the excerpt for the mocking vein:

> I talked to him about the wisdom of my village—half repeating things. I remembered Granny saying, and half making things up on the spot—and he nodded. It was a scene to put you in mind of that passage in the *Bhagavad Gita*, when our Lord Krishna—another of history's famous chauffeurs—stops the chariot he is driving and gives his passenger some excellent advice on life and death. Like Krishna I philosophised—I joked—I even sang a song—all to make Mr Ashok feel better. (*The White Tiger* 187)

For him, Mr. Ashok seems to be a baby, "big, pathetic baby" who is calmed down with the soothing words. But, somewhere, he realises that he takes pleasure in the pathetic condition of his master whom he wishes to see suffer. He presents it philosophically:

> It squeezed my heart to see him suffer like this—but where my genuine concern for him ended and where my self-interest began, I could not tell: no servant can ever tell what the motives of his heart are.
>
> Do we loathe our masters behind a façade of love—or do we love them behind a facade of loathing?
>
> We are made mysteries to ourselves by the Rooster Coop we are locked in.
>
> (*The White Tiger* 187)

Whether it is hatred for the master inwardly that comes out in the form of love or love for the master that comes out in the form of hatred, he feels perplexed to the extent that he thinks himself to be mysterious.

It is surprising that, later in life, when he settles in Bangalore and becomes the white tiger, he does not think of a prayer for his ex-master Mr Ashok though he uses his name for him. He thinks that "there was no need to offer a prayer to the gods for him, because his family would be offering very expensive prayer all along the Ganga for his soul. What can a poor man's prayers mean to the 36,000,004 gods in comparison with those of the rich." (*The White Tiger* 316-17)? Ironically he calls himself poor and a poor man's prayer will be of no use to Mr Ashok. He thinks about his murder, misses him and feels that he did not deserve such a fate from his hand. Though at one place he admits that he should have murdered Mongoose in place of Mr. Ashok, he will never say that he committed a mistake when he murdered his master because of his strong desire not to feel like a servant.

When Balram takes his weight on the machine, it releases a slip that weighs him 59 with the line "Respect for the law is the first command of the gods" (*The White Tiger* 248). The machine is again a means to limit the freedom and, hence, works as a coop at the juncture when he is to board the train to begin a new life. Mark the mental state of Balram Halwai:

> I let the fortune-telling chit fall on the floor and I laughed. Even here, in the weight machine of a train station, they try to hoodwink us. Here, on the threshold of man's freedom, just before he boards a train to a new life, there flashing fortune machines are the final alarm bell of the Rooster Coop. (*The White Tiger* 248)

The machine also speaks of the language of gods programmed by man, the master, so that man may respect law and not think of his freedom from the rooster coop.

Adiga makes Balram poke fun at religion and great men like Gandhi. He makes the Chinese Premier understand that this is India where bribery and corruption are done with the approval of great men and religion. Everywhere the portraits of Ganesh, Saraswati and Lakshmi, along with one great man Gandhi are seen in the offices and drawing rooms where bribery is given or taken. Portraits on the wall also approve the action while the reality is that no religion allows bribery, and as to Gandhi, he never took bribe in his life-time. Gandhi now has become the symbol of wealth because of his image on the currency and also on the walls of the office. Mark the passage that mockingly presents the way Balram Halwai offers a bribe in the police office where the three portraits of gods and one of Gandhi witness the scene:

> Behind him were three portraits of gods. But not the one I was looking for.
>
> Oh, thank God. There was one of Gandhi too. It was in the corner.
>
> With a big smile—and a Namaste—I handed him the red bag. He opened it cautiously.
>
> We sipped cup after cup of steaming coffee under a calendar that had the face of the goddess Lakshmi on it—she was showering gold coins from a pot into the river of prosperity. Above her was a framed portrait of the god of gods, a grinning Mahatma Gandhi.
>
> (*The White Tiger* 310)

Mockingly he calls Gandhi god of gods. He asks the Chinese Premier not to go to the Ganga and ashrams but to the National zoo in New Delhi where he can learn a lot. He is surprised why thousands of foreigners go to the Himalayas, or to Benaras or to Bodh Gaya for enlightenment. These foreigners think that they are enlightened if "they get into weird poses of yoga, smoke hashish, shag a sadhu or two" (*The White Tiger* 275). For them, India seems to be a place where sadhus are homosexual and smoking hashish will lead them to the way to the other world. Yoga, deep breathing and meditation are the only means that help a lot in relaxing the mind and widening the vision necessary for "the perfect start to the entrepreneur's day" (*The White Tiger* 292). On the basis of his own experience of handling the stresses of business with the help of yoga, he suggests to the Chinese Premier to "make yoga a must in all Chinese schools" (*The White Tiger* 292).

Adiga makes fun of Hindu religion vehemently, speaks in a suppressed voice against Muslim but nowhere he speaks against Buddhism except at one place where he says: "It's when your driver starts to read about Gandhi and the Buddha that it's time to wet your pants, Mr Jiabao" (126). It seems that he is afraid of China where he plans to secure his future as he thinks that the future lies with the brown and yellow people. He is sure that the Premier might have heard the name of Bodh Gaya where "the Lord Buddha sat under a tree and found his enlightenment and started Buddhism, which then spread to the whole world, including China" (*The White Tiger* 18). But, he himself lives at Laxmangarh, a place which is just a few miles far from Bodh Gaya, and even today the place is full of darkness. In the school, the teacher has spoilt all the walls with the spitting of *paan* except one that has "A faded mural of the Lord Buddha surrounded by deer and squirrels" (*The White Tiger* 29). Balram is afraid of the lizard, the only animal at the feet of the Lord Buddha. Why does Adiga not speak against Buddhism? Does he wish to please the Chinese Premier?

Balram Halwai's role model is Vijay, the opportunist whom he appreciates and wishes to emulate. Whenever opportunities knock at his door, he welcomes them and does not let them go—whether it is of getting job, or of getting an upper hand on the Nepali guard, or removing Ram Persad or murdering his master or stealing the money, etc. For him there is no god except success, even at the cost of consciousness or religion. He is a Hindu outwardly but inwardly a Marxist who searches for ways to make fun of religion. When he is about to finish his story which he narrates through the letters to the Chinese Premier, he gives him a hint that reflects his Marxist mindset. He plans to sell everything and begins an English language school for poor children in Bangalore, to whom he will teach the facts of life. He will not fill their heads with religion or great men like Gandhi. He will turn these children into white tigers—tigers that will speak the language of science and technology and not of religion. It will be his ideal communism—a place where religion will not be known and people will know only facts. There will be no rooster coop like religion or family to stop their growth. Mark the excerpt for the ideal that he wishes to translate into reality:

> After three or four years in real estate, I think I might sell everything, take the money, and start a school—an English-language school—for poor children in Bangalore. A school where you won't be allowed to corrupt anyone's head with prayers and stories about God or Gandhi—nothing but the facts of life for these kids. A school full of White tigers, unleashed on Bangalore! We'd have this city at our knees, I tell you. I could become the Boss of Bangalore. I'd fix that assistant commissioner of police at once. I'd put him on a bicycle and have Asif knock him over it with the Qualis. (*The White Tiger* 319-20)

What will be the future of such a school and the students that he wishes to teach? For him, relationship is meaningless. What will happen? Is he not leading the state into anarchy where there will be the rule of 'might is right'? Murder a man to become a man. What a philosophy! It seems that the crazy Balram Halwai needs the lesson of Hindu ethics that will eliminate his "mental impurities" like "greed and egotism, for the ultimate attainment of the highest good" (*Hinduism* 68).

How far will Madras (Chennai) born Adiga with dual citizenship—of India and Australia—display the derogatory image of India in the name of self-examination? What is he going to prove with this picture? What has he got is the name and fame along with the Booker Prize? The spectacles of rationalism make him see that India is not a place to live in. Has he forgotten the ancient heritage? Has he forgotten that this India had been a golden bird that attracted various foreigners? Does he not see that today the people of the world seek peace and inspiration from Gandhi while for him Gandhi is a useless commodity? To him it may not be an attack on the country but to every sensible Indian it is a slaughter of culture for the sake of pleasing the West or the Chinese Premier by displaying the naked picture of spiritually rich India.

No doubt, India is on the global map and attracts the greater powers that see her as the future market for their goods. It is a land where mother Ganga flows and where

Buddha received enlightenment. He must be thankful to God that he is born in India. Though, in the beginning, he makes Balram Halwai read before inspector that "*We live in a glorious land. The Lord Buddha received his enlightenment in this land. The River Ganga gives life to our plants and our animals and our people. We are grateful to God that we were born in this land*' (*The White Tiger* 34), later he changes his mind that results in a robot which rationalises everything on the scale of utility before taking any final decision, and for this even murder of the master is permissible. What will happen when a more rationalised and professional man will meet Balram Halwai whom he will kill to become the boss and then another with more power? When will the struggle for power come to an end? When will man be a man in the real sense? He wishes to make a species of man that does not believe in religion, family and moral values. Human relationship, if not useful, is meaningless. All these things reveal that Adiga is somewhere a patient of inner sickness. What he needs is what he has discarded. Certainly it is religion that can bring back to him his healthy mental state which will make him realise that "it is not religion that is responsible for hatred and cruelty, but human bigotry and narrowness" (*Hinduism* 180). He must realise the importance of religion that gives "equanimity of mind in prosperity and adversity, courage to face the problems of his life, and a vision of his ultimate spiritual destiny" (*Hinduism* 19). He should not forget that it is not the time to dissect one's religion but it's high time when India needs his intelligence and talent for suggesting ways of fighting against terrorism, a monster that intends to swallow the world. Religion is not the root cause of evil, rather it is a force that binds the people into one thread and, moreover, no religion teaches to defame and speak ill-will against other religions. Hence, according to Nikhilananada, "the world's malady is spiritual. Suspicion, ill-will, far, and greed, which have been poisoning human relationships, are the symptoms of an inner sickness. For the world's recovery the root of this sickness must be removed. Religion alone can accomplish the cure by generating in men the power of aggressive goodness necessary to fight aggressive evil" (*Hinduism* 15).

Works Cited

Adiga, Aravind. *The White Tiger*. New Delhi: HarperCollins, 2008. **Print.**

Nehru, Jawahar Lal. *The Discovery of India*. New Delhi: Asia Publishing House, 1960 (New Impression). **Print.**

Nikhilananda, Swami. *Hinduism Its Meaning for the Liberation of the Spirit*. Madras: Sri Ramakrishna Math, 1982, second edition. (First in 1968). **Print.**

3

The Black River

For Aravind Adiga, the Ganga is not a holy river; it is simply a drain where, to take a dip, will be a dangerous step. He uses the abusive words for mother Ganga to make the Chinese Premier believe that it is not the holy river where sins can be washed away and where having a dip can offer him calm of mind. Before coming to his version of the Ganga, let us see what Nehru says: "The story of the Ganges, from her source to the sea, from old times to new, is the story of India's civilisation and culture, of the rise and fall of empires, of great and proud cities, of the adventure of man and the quest of the mind which has so occupied India's thinkers, of the richness and fulfilment of life as well as its denial and renunciation, of ups and downs, of growth and decay, of life and death" (*The Discovery of India* 38). For Nehru, the story of India's civilisation and culture is the story of the flow of the Ganges.

Mark the words of Swami Tapovan for the importance of the Ganga in shaping the destiny of India: "She is 'Mother of the Universe,' as She looks after the people of Bharata, as a mother would look after her children. She nurses and nourishes the Gangetic Valley and but for Her icy-cold perennial stream the Rajputana desert would have by now spread over to Delhi and even up north. Lastly, it is in Her valleys, up in the mountains, that the Rishis sat, lived, reflected and contemplated upon, and soared in their meditations to heights of thinking, the altitudes of which have not yet been, even from afar, touched by any human generation ever after, anywhere.

And it is again the Gangetic Valley of the North-Indian plains that the glorious Aryans selected to settle down, to live the Hindu Culture and grow, proper and achieve a brilliant civilisation of Peace, Love and Progress" (I:1).

The river Ganga is the life-breath for Nehru and Tapovan but to Adiga, it is the end of breath of life. On the basis of this river and ocean, he makes a division of India—India of Darkness and India of Light. The river symbolises the darkness while the ocean brings light. For him the south is a place of light. The cities that are near to the sea are full of light—light of knowledge and light of prosperity with modern amenities. The Ganga, no doubt, for him, has made the northern part—the cowbelt—anarea of darkness. It is the area that covers Uttar Pradesh and Bihar which, for Adiga, are the most backward states where caste-syndrome has spread like plague, where the python of feudalism swallows the poor; where corruption has become oxygen, where superstitions have become the way of life and where the holy water of the Ganga is still a miracle for purifying sins. It is "a fertile place" which is "full of rice fields and wheat fields" and the people who live here call it "the darkness". He makes the Premier understand that "India is two countries in one: an India of Light, and an India of Darkness. The ocean brings light to my country. Every place on the map of India near the ocean is well-off. But the river brings darkness to India—the black river" (*The White Tiger* 14).

How can the Ganga bring darkness when she makes the land fertile? To call the Ganga black river seems to be not only a hoax but also a conspiracy to play with the religious feelings of the Hindus. His hatred for the Ganga does not cease here. He crosses all the limits and calls it a river of death, Yamaraj, the lord of Death that takes everything in its grip. Mark the disparaging terms that he uses for the mother Ganga: "Which black river am I talking of–which river of Death, whose banks are full of rich, dark, sticky mud whose grip traps everything that is planted in it, suffocating and choking and stunting it" (*The White Tiger* 15)?

Adiga ironically appreciates the Ganga calling her "Mother Ganga, daughter of the Vedas, river of illumination, protector of us all, breaker of the chain of birth and rebirth" (*The White Tiger* 15). But, the next moment, he declares that "Everywhere this river flows, that area is the Darkness" (*The White Tiger* 15). How can the river of illumination bring darkness to the area? This river, being "the river of emancipation" (*The White Tiger* 15) attracts, for Adiga, not the Indians all over the country but hundreds of American tourists who "come each year to take photographs of naked *sadhus* at Hardwar or Benaras" (*The White Tiger* 15). Again, what a joke! It seems absurd to think that Americans, after spending a lot of money, come to India only to take the photographs of the naked *sadhus*.

Adiga, through his protagonist Balram Halwai, suggests to the Chinese Premier not to take a bath in the river Ganga because of the pollution. For him, the river seems to be full of faeces and dead bodies. It seems that the industrial acids have been poured into the river knowingly. Mark the abusive language that he uses for the mother Ganga to make the Premier believe that it is not the holy river where sins will be washed away and where having a dip will give him calm of mind: "No!—Mr Jiabao, I urge you not to dip in the Ganga, unless you want your mouth full of faeces, straw, soggy parts of human bodies, buffalo carrion, and seven different kinds of industrial acids" (*The White Tiger* 15).

Is the river herself responsible for the industrial acids and faeces? Has she asked man like him to pour such things or is man responsible for the pollution? Adiga's chief aim is to demean the holy Ganga and shock the people who have faith in her healing power. If he is really conscious of the environmental pollution, why does he not talk of any action plan for her purification? He seems to be a nihilist blabber when he presents the derogatory picture of the Ganga. Tapovan criticises such people, calling them self-deceived, if they believe that their blabbing will lessen the faith of the people in the miraculous charm of the river Ganga. While invoking her, he states:

> Let the Nihilists blabber
> that Thou art
> "Non-Existent!"
> Let the unintelligent ones
> insult and demean Thee!
> They get themselves
> only self-deceived.
> O *Sat-Chit-Ghana*!
> In spite of
> all these,
> Thy devotees
> will never
> turn their eyes
> away from Thee! (III: 6)

Balram, the protagonist, goes to the river for cremation of his dead mother. He smells the river from afar and declares that it is the only truth. It seems that he makes his impression with his nose, not with his eyes. Mark the excerpt: "I smelled the river before I saw it: a stench of decaying flesh rising from my right. I sang louder: '...the only truth!" (16). The stench of flesh that enters his nose from afar makes him believe that it is the river of death, not of life. This is the river that swallows everything through its mud. For him, the Ganga is not *Ganga maiya* but a she-devil that swallows man. He becomes so apprehensive that he imagines his own death and the rites that would follow soon. Mark the lines for his apprehensive nature: "And then I understood: this was the real god of Benaras—this black mud of the Ganga into which everything died, and decomposed, and was reborn from, and died into again. The same would happen to me when I died and they brought me here. Nothing would get liberated here" (*The White Tiger* 18).

No sooner does he imagine his death than he faints. He fears so much that he decides not to go to the Ganga thereafter and leaves "that river for the American tourists" (*The White Tiger* 18). Whether it happened due to the cremation on the bank of the Ganga or not, somehow, he developed a sort of antipathy for her. Every Hindu longs for his death on the bank of the Ganga. Her water is *gangajal* used for the purpose of purification. Every dying Hindu wishes for some drops of the *gangajal*. His denouncing Ganga reveals his transformation from a theist to an atheist. But, his denouncing cannot smash the faith of the Hindus. Tapovan declares that those who do not believe in the existence of the Ganga as a holy river are atheists. Balram Halwai is such an atheist.

Let the atheists declare:

> "Thou art not."
> for the same reasons
> for which
> the owls hoot:
> "There is no Sun." (Tapovan III: 25)

Balram Halwai is, indeed, an owl that hoots and denies the existence of the Ganga as a sacred river. His demeaning nature does not stop here. Even the area near the Ganga is equally satirised as he thinks that the people who work here never grow up. Mark the excerpt: "Go to a tea shop anywhere along the Ganga, sir, and look at the men working in that tea shop – men, I say, but better to call them human spiders that go crawling in between and under the tables with rags in their hands, crushed humans in crushed uniforms, sluggish, unshaven, in their thirties or forties or fifties but still 'boys' (*The White Tiger* 51). Men who work near the Ganga do not seem to be men but human spiders. They become insects for him not because they are workers or servants but because of their association with his Ganga, the river that he hates somewhere even at his subconscious level. He is so much obsessed with his hatred for the Ganga that even when he learns driving and the things related with it, this river is also present in his mind. Mark the excerpt for his own depiction as a pig from a sewage and his dipping into a black Ganga: "I emerged from under a taxi like a pig from sewage, my face black with grease, my hands shiny with engine oil. I dipped into a Ganga of black—and came out a driver" (*The White Tiger* 57). When he thinks of his marriage and children, the river Ganga is not absent from his mind. Whom a man hates most keeps always remembering in spite of his determined intention of forgetting. He hates the Ganga to the extent that in spite of his attempt he never forgets her.

Balram Halwai feels that he is a part "of all that is changing this country" and thinks that he has done a lot for poor men who will not make an end of their lives while rotting in the black mud of Mother Ganga. Again, the excerpt shows that he is hypocrite to the core in his attitude towards the Ganga whom he calls Mother. The truth is otherwise. "Why not? Am I not a part of all that is changing this country? Haven't I succeeded in the struggle that every poor man here should be making –the struggle not to take the lashes your father took, not to end up in a mound of indistinguishable bodies that will rot in the black mud of Mother Ganga" (*The White Tiger* 318)?

There are two good sentences that have come out from Adiga's ironical pen. Balram Halwai whose nose, because of its capacity for smelling the stench, works better than eyes which do not see anything except faeces and swimming half-burnt dead bodies. But, sometimes, his mind's eyes are able to see what his physical eyes fail to do. His mind's eye sees an island of white sand which shines brighter because of the sunlight. He imagines that his mother's soul might have gone here to take rest. Mark the lines for the beauty of description: "In the distance, an island of white sand glistened in the sunlight, and boats full of people were heading to that island. I wondered if my mother's soul had flown there, to that shining place in the river" (*The White Tiger* 17). It is the love of Halwai for his mother that he imagines a heavenly abode glisten with sunlight while seeing the white sand. As the river is associated with the deliverance, somehow, his mind's eye imagines what the physical eyes fail to see. Except these two lines in *The White Tiger*, there is nothing which can add to the glory of the Mother Ganga. He has attempted to debunk the myth of the Ganga as a sacred river that emancipates all the people who take a holy bath.

The Ganga, known as Bhagirthi because of Bhagirath who brought her on earth for the deliverance of his ancestors, has become polluted not of her own but because of the materialistic attitude of man who has exploited her to the maximum for his benefit, irrespective of the acid and poisonous stuff that he pours into her flow. India has her own identity because of the *rishis* and *munis* who got enlightenment on her bank. It is the Ganga who has kept the Indian cultural heritage alive, and writers like Adiga who are after name and fame even at the cost of belittling the national pride do not hesitate in depicting her as the black river that knows only how to embrace death. Will the Booker Prize-winner Adiga come down from the sky on earth to take a dip in the river Ganga? Will he dip his pen in the ink that may recommend some measures to stop pollution? Has he not any desire somewhere lurking in any corner of his heart to be cremated on her bank? Does his conscience not feel guilty while playing with the religious feelings? Does the white tiger have any courage to awake the people who knowingly pollute her for their material gains? Will the white tiger remain in the foreign jungle full of amenities? Will he not come to the plains and see with eyes that millions of people come here to take a bath that gives them mental peace? Who is right—whether the white tiger with the Western specs or the millions of people? No doubt, the white tiger knows the truth but remains silent because in spite of its own desire for designing action plan for removing pollution, it cannot do so as the Western jungle will not allow him to enter.

Works Cited

Adiga, Aravind. *The White Tiger*. New Delhi: HarperCollins, 2008. **Print.**

Nehru, Jawaharlal. *The Discovery of India*. New Delhi: Asia Publishing House, 1960 (New Impression). **Print**.

Tapovan, Swami. *Hymn to Ganga (Gangstotram)*. Trans. & Commentary by Chimaya. Uttarkashi: Tapovan Kuti, 1969. **Print**.

4

Reversing the Script

Aravind Adiga's *The White Tiger* roars so loud that its roaring can be heard even from a distance. Going through the novel gives a shock to the follower of the Indian heritage and culture. The novel seems to be simple though it is not so because of the well-crafted allegory that uncovers itself only on the repeated readings. The language is simple but not the ideas that become the mess for the reader who attempts to decode them to know the novelist's intention. It is a well-constructed and preconceived novel based on the communist ideology. As it is based on a particular ideology, it becomes biased to some traditional and cultural legacies. On a deeper level, it seems to reverse the Hindus' religious book, the *Ramayana*. Adiga has done it intentionally because of the communist ideology that rejects religion considering it simply opium. To shock the cultural heritage, it reverses the script of the *Ramayana*. He dips his pen in satire and then writes to counteract the teachings and ideals of the *Ramayana*. It is to Adiga, the so-called Westernised Valmiki who shows the victory of evil over good to oppose the victory of good over evil. He transforms the monkey into the white tiger who establishes his own *Ramrajya* where morality has no meaning.

Here begins the critique of Aravind Adiga's The *Ramayana*, titled *The White Tiger*.

Adiga's hero Balram Halwai prays to the High Power for the success of telling the story known as 'The Autobiography of a Half-Baked Indian' to the Chinese Premier.

In India, it is a part of the culture that one begins any work with the prayer to one's own *ishta devta* or *devi*. Balram guesses that he "should start off by kissing some god's arse" (8) but is not sure which god as there are 36,000,004 divine arses and so folds his hands "in a reverent Namaste" (9) to pray to all the arses completing it in no time. He is half-educated as he was taken out of the school because of adverse circumstances that sprang up due to the loan taken from the Stork for the marriage. As a boy he differentiates himself from other students by virtue of his intelligence and gets the title of the 'white tiger' from the school inspector. It is not his fault that this incomplete education makes him kiss the arses, not the feet. What can one expect from Balram with two-three years of schooling that can make him "read and write" but not be able to understand what he has read? Mr Ashok calls him "half-baked" (10) but in India, those who are half-baked dominate over the fully-baked. The full-baked receive the order from the half-baked. To be a successful entrepreneur, one does not need high education but the guts which a half-baked always has. This half-baked Balram Halwai considers himself the monkey Hanuman but just performs the activities quite contrary to the nature of Hanuman.

Balram Halwai and his creator Aravind Adiga can find the hierarchy among gods who fight for their survival in India and make their boundary line through the river Ganga. The area of the river Ganga is the area of darkness which is dominated by the deity Hanuman, the hero of everyone in the village. Valmiki has taught the lesson of devotion and service through the example of Hanuman. It is Hanuman who is always called forth at the hour of crisis. Adiga sees here a net that is woven to enwrap villagers so that they may remain servants throughout their lives. He forgets or intentionally avoids the fact that the worship of Hanuman is not confined to the villages as even the landlords and others also worship Hanuman for knowledge, strength and intelligence.

Balram Halwai secures the job of chauffeur in the Stork family. He gets an opportunity to go to Delhi with Mr Ashok and his wife Pinky Madam whom he regards as Ram and Sita respectively. He takes them to the places where they like and feels the same feelings as was felt by Hanuman while carrying Ram and Sita on his shoulders. Pinky Madam who is like the image of the goddess in Birla Temple is Sita for him.

When the other driver, Ram Persad, chants 'Om, Om, Om' and prays bowing his head before the pictures of various gods, he asks Balram whether he prays or not. To show his fidelity and devotion to counteract Ram Persad, he goes to the market and brings "two dozen of the cheapest idols of Hanuman and Ram". Now, with Ram Persad, he competes in prayers. It was Hanuman who opened his chest and showed Ram and Sita therein in order to show his devotion to them. Here, Balram shows his devotion not thorough his work but through the cheapest idols which he has brought from the market. He prays as a reaction to Ram Persad and so his prayer is not genuine. He shows that his masters are like his parents. How can he think of taking any money for his service from the master? When Mr Mukesh asks him how much rupees he will take, he responds with devotion saying: "Absolutely nothing, sir. You're like a father and mother to me, and how can I ask for money from my parents" (65)?

This Balram is a modernised Hanuman who believes in consumerism and, hence, makes Vijay, the icon of victory, his ideal. He walks on every path without considering right or wrong because he thinks that a path that leads to success is the right path for him. Vijay is his childhood hero, one who climbed the steps of success right from his beginning with the job of bus conductor to a politician. As a child he wishes for the uniform and the whistle so that he may look like a dominating personality. When he gets the job and uniform, his happiness knows no bounds. Later, his longings for power and pelf take him away from the right path turning him from a faithful servant to a traitor who murders his master Mr Ashok and takes his place declaring himself as a North Indian entrepreneur.

Pinky Madam, whom Balram regards as Sita, uses abusive words in her talks. Sita, an ideal for women, teaches not to speak harsh words to anyone. Here, for Pinky Madam, everything is 'fucking'. She uses abusive phrases like "What a fucking joke" (7). Not to talk of Hanuman, even Lakshman never saw the full face of Sita and when Ravana takes her away, she throws the ornaments so that Rama may guess her whereabouts. Lakshman sees the bangles but says that he has touched the feet of Sita and can recognise the ornaments of her feet. That was the character of Valmiki's Sita. What is the character of this modern Sita of Balram Halwai? Pinky Madam does not mind playing badminton with her servants in her trousers. She comes to Balram's quarter and knocks at the door. He is surprised to see her with two rackets in her hands. The net is tied and both Pinky Madam and Balram take their sides. She hits the shuttle which rises up but he fails to respond and, hence, it falls near his foot. Mark the conversation that makes Balram feel the inferiority in the game:

> 'Hey! Move! Hit it back!'
>
> 'Sorry, Madam. I'm so sorry.'
>
> I'd never played this game before. I hit the shuttle back to her, and it went straight into the net.
>
> 'Oh, you're *useless*. Where is that other driver?' (77)

Pinky Madam calls Balram 'useless', a word that certainly makes him angry from inside with the feeling why he does not know how to play badminton. When he sees Ram Persad responding to her shot for shot, he is filled with hatred for him and asks himself: "Is there any hatred on earth like the hatred of the number two servant for the number one" (77)?

For Hanuman, Sita is the mother and, so, impure thoughts never enter his mind. That's why he is so loved and worshipped among people who seek inspiration of purity and strength from him. He is a true *bhakta* who has Rama and Sita in his heart. Here, Aravind Adiga's Hanuman Balram Halwai is corrupt mentally because of his fantasy and lust for Pinky Madam and the things associated with her. She wears short skirts and when Mr Mukesh goes away, the skirts become "even shorter". He sees Pinky Madam and "half her boobs hanging out of her clothes" (143) through the rearview mirror. The scene of her boobs puts him in a bad situation to the extent that his 'beak' arises out of passion. But, how can he "get excited by the mistress" (143) when she is like his mother Sita and the wife of his master Mr Ashok? He thinks that he will not look at the rearview mirror to avoid such situations though he confesses: "If there was a crash, it wouldn't be my fault" (143). Her low black dress makes his 'beak' big. He develops a kind of hatred for the dress but hates his 'beak' because of its erection. He is in the moral dilemma and fails to decide what he should do. Being a healthy man, erection is natural. Pinky Madam is young and beautiful but she is the wife of the master and the master is like father. The wife of the father is a mother and with a mother, not to talk of having sex, he cannot imagine such a thing.

She comes and asks him whether he can make "some traditional type of ginger tea" (145) for her. Though he has no idea, he says yes and feels relief because of her covered boobs. But, this American Sita not only takes the ginger tea but also loves to take wine. She takes English liquor and asks him to give him the steering wheel. But, Mr Ashok asks him not to give the steering because of her drunkard state. She scolds him and states: "What a fucking joke! Everyone in India drinks and drives. But you won't let *me* do it" (159). She forces him to stop while Mr Ashok asks him to drive. Their clashing longings leave him confused as he does not wish to make anyone angry. He takes the car five feet in front of the white line and then stops. Mr Ashok appreciates him calling his action "pretty clever" while Pinky Madam compliments him saying: Yes, Ashok. He's a fucking genius" (160).

Once, Pinky Madam leaves Balram, dressed as Maharaja on the road, and drives but later she comes and asks him whether he is not angry. He simply says that "Employers are like mother and father. How can one be angry with them" (162)? She mocks and mocks but he remains calm and says nothing. But, when she scolds him for his teeth and his bad habit of scratching his groin, he feels so insulted that he develops an inferiority complex and feels angry with his dead father for not teaching him the civilised way. Mark the excerpt for Pinky Madam's insulting behaviour towards Balram:

> 'What are you doing?' she shouted.
>
> 'Washing ginger, madam.'
>
> 'That's with your right hand. What's your left hand doing?'
>
> 'Madam?'
>
> I looked down.
>
> 'Stop scratching your groin with your left hand!'

> 'Don't be angry, madam. I'll stop.'
>
> But it was no use. She would not stop shouting:
>
> 'You're a filthy! Look at you, look at your teeth, look at your clothes! There's red *paan* all over you teeth, and there are red spots on your shirt. It's disgusting! Get out—clean up the mess you've made in the kitchen and get out.' (146)

The way she rebukes and insults directly strikes his inner being. The incident of hit-and-run case breaks him to the extent that he begins to develop a hatred for his master and mistress. Once, she drinks too much, takes the steering from Balram and hits a poor boy. Balram is sacrificed in the name of faithfulness and devotion to the family. He is held responsible for the crime that he has not committed. But, somehow, Pinky Madam's sleeping conscience awakes and, then, she decides to go to the family of the victim. "Who would have thought, Mr Jiabao, that of this whole family, this lady with the short skirts would be the one with a conscience" (180)? The Stork does not like her behaviour and thinks that "she's gone crazy" (180). The Stork asks his Rama-like son to have control over his wife in a better way.

Rama was exiled for 14 years because of Kaikayi who wished to make her son the king of Ayodhya. But, Bharat did not accept the kingdom and waited for the return of his brother Rama. Here, Mr Ashok is sent to America for study but returns with his wife Pinky Madam. He marries her against the wishes of his father. Pinky Madam, who is Sita for Balram, feels a fish out of water in India. She comes to India with the expectation that she will return to America after three months. When she asks Mr Ashok for the date of return and does not get a satisfactory response, she begins to cry and starts quarrelling with him.

> 'You lied about returning to America, didn't you, Ashok?—you're never going back, are you?'
>
> 'There's a driver in the car, Pinky—I'll explain everything later.'
>
> 'Oh, what does he matter! He's only the driver. And you're just changing the topic again!' (81)

In Valmiki's *Ramayana*, it was Sita who happily lived with Rama in exile. Sita feels she is in heaven there where her Rama is. Here, Mr Ashok plans to settle in India because of all the facilities that he gets here. For him, India is America now and even better than America where no servant serves morning tea when one is in bed. Here, Pinky Madam does not like to live in India and forces Mr Ashok to return.

In the *Ramayana*, Sita is abducted by Ravana who takes her to his Lanka where he puts her under the custody of the *rakshasas* and *rakshassni*. She weeps there because she cannot live without Rama. When Rama comes to know about her capture, he becomes sad. Then, Hanuman is sent to know her whereabouts. Hanuman crosses the ocean and reaches Lanka where he finds Sita in her miserable condition. He gives her a ring to make her believe that he has been sent by Rama. It is Hanuman who tells Rama and Sita about each other's welfare. But, here, Adiga has written a new script. The role of Hanuman has become different. Now, he will separate the pair. This action will bring freedom for Pinky Madam but it will make Mr Ashok weak to the extent that he will begin to drink too much. Here is a scene, when Pinky Madam comes to this Hanuman.

> When I woke up, someone was standing in my room, turning the lights on and off.
>
> It was Pinky Madam.
>
> 'Get ready. You're going to drive me.'
>
> 'Yes, madam,' I said, rubbing my eyes. 'What time is it?'
>
> She put a finger to her lips.
>
> I put on a shirt, and then got the car out, and drove it to the front of the building. She had a bag in her hand.
>
> 'Where to?' I asked. It was two in the morning.
>
> She told me, and I asked, 'Isn't Sir coming?'
>
> 'Just drive.'
>
> I drove her to the airport, I asked no questions.

> When she got out at the airport, she pushed a brown envelope into my window—then slammed her door and left.
>
> And that was how, Your Excellency, my employer's marriage came to an end. (181)

This Hanuman does not give Sita his master's ring but receives from her a brown envelope containing money. He does not think of informing his master even for a second though he simply asks her about the coming of the master. Finally, the driver drives her to the airport, the place that will show her the way to her emancipation. Sita has come out from Rama's jail. Here, for her, her husband is not Rama but Ravana. It is Balram Halwai who embraces the role of Hanuman and becomes the emancipator for her. Pinky Madam has got freedom to live and her parents are also "happy with her decision" (188). The moment Mr Ashok comes to know that Pinky Madam has gone forever and Balram drove her to the airport, he loses his control and abuses him calling him "sister-fucker". He quarrels with him and pushes him against the balcony but Balram gathers courage and kicks his master. He shouts at his master and asks him not to blame him wholly because he has "never heard of a woman leaving her husband forever" (182). He simply did what she ordered. A crow sees the quarrel between the two and simply caws to make its presence feel. "A crow sat down on the balcony and cawed. Both of us turned and stared at it" (182). The presence of the crow again takes the reader to the *Ramayana*.

Jatayu tries to save Sita from the clutches of Ravana who, with his sword-clips the wings. Here, the crow simply caws as it has no role to save Sita. It is natural that when someone's wife goes away or leaves her husband, people will talk about the affair. Pinky Madam's going to America becomes a hot topic among drivers who ask him strange questions regarding the relationship of Pinky Madam and Mr Ashok. But, he simply says that "the gate keeper has gone blind" (183) and nothing else. The other drivers call him "loyal to the last" (183).

As soon as Pinky Madam goes, Mr Ashok becomes disappointed and frustrated. He gives way to immorality and debauchery which become a bog. He runs after beautiful prostitutes and enjoys sex with them but the physical pleasure does not give him inner satisfaction. He enjoys sex with a Ukrainian student but when he returns, he seems to be ill because of the failure of an emotional bond. Balram who is outside imagines that his master will come running, asking him to save him but nothing happens. Mr Ashok shares with Balram that he has no courage to change the way of his life because he has no "balls" (237). He allowed the people to exploit him and never complained. He never could do what he longed for. This makes him believe that his master has no courage while he himself is a man of courage. The weak point of his master allures him to take the place of the master. Mr Sharma wishes to eat the common food. The scene of eating food reminds one of Sabri who offered the plums to Shri Rama who ate them with satisfaction.

> 'Order for us, Balram. Order the commoners' food.'
>
> I ordered okra, cauliflower, radish, spinach, and *dhal*. Enough to feed a whole family, or one rich man.
>
> He ate and burped and ate some more.
>
> 'This food is fantastic. And just twenty-five rupees! You people eat so well!'
>
> When he was done, I ordered him a *lassi*, and when he took the first sip, he smiled. 'I like eating your kind of food!'
>
> I smiled and thought, *I like eating your kind of food too*. (238)

It is surprising that Mr Ashok likes the common food while Balram thinks of the food of the rich man. Eating the common food gives Balram further a clue of Mr Ashok who is a man with weak determination. A man with weak determination is soon wiped out in the struggle for existence. It also makes him believe that he is powerful and a powerful man is serving the weak one. He is serving him because he is rich. Why can he not be rich? Why can he not become Mr Ashok Sharma himself? Hanuman-like Balram becomes ambitious and this ambition makes him take a decision in spite of the moral dilemma. With Pinky Madam, Mr Ashok was strong. Without her he is weak, a simple man who can be easily killed. When he is drunk and does not awake, Balram slaps him on the face so that he may get up. He slaps him again and thinks that "slapping the master when he's asleep" is a "time-honoured servants' tradition" (184).

Rama's brother Bharat did not agree to rule over Ayodhya in favour of Rama. Mukesh, the Mongoose, and Mr Ashok return after bribing the ministers. Somehow, Mukesh feels that his one rupee coin is lost. This Bharat-like brother makes Balram search for the lost coin. Mark the way Mr Mukesh orders him to search for the coin:

> 'Get down on your knees. Look for it on the floor of the car.'
>
> I got down on my knees. I sniffed in between the mats like a dog, all in search of that one rupee.
>
> 'What do you mean, it's not there? Don't think you can steal from us just because you're in the city. I want that rupee.'
>
> 'We've just paid half a million rupees in a bribe, Mukesh, and now we're screwing this man over for a single rupee. Let's go up and have a scotch.'
>
> 'That's how you corrupt servants. It starts with one rupee. Don't bring your American ways here.'
>
> Where that rupee coin went remains a mystery to me to this day, Mr Premier. Finally, I took a rupee coin out of my shirt pocket, dropped it on the floor of the car, picked it up, and gave it to the Mongoose. (139)

Though Mr Ashok asks him not to think about the coin, he is not ready to be satisfied until he gets it. Hanuman might not have so much difficulty in searching for the *sanjivini buti* as Balram faced. When he fails to search, he takes his own coin from the pocket and hands it over to Mr Mukesh who feels a childlike satisfaction. But, this behaviour from Mr Mukesh humiliates him so much that he feels a kind of rage in him and this rage comes out in the form of Mr Ashok's murder.

Now, Balram plans to be the master and searches for the way to translate it. Why is he not Rama? He is not so simply because he has no money. Who has money? Where is the money? It is in the hands of capitalists or landowners. He imagines a man in the khaki uniform who spits at God. This spitting is the spitting on the moral values that he now determines to leave. He goes to the side of Satan in order to rule like a master. First, he has to search out the way to kill Ravana to beçome Rama. For this Hanuman, Rama becomes Ravana. He finds the secret and the secret lies in the red bag with money. This is *amrit*, the nectar that Mr Ashok is distributing to the *rakshasas* in Delhi while in the real sense it belongs to the ordinary people. Hence, he thinks of stealing this nectar which is in the red bag. But, he will have to kill Ravana who possesses it. He takes out arrows and hits them on him. The arrow is sharp in the form of "a good, strong bottle, Johnnie Walker Black" (285). He hits the bottle three times on Mr Ashok's head to smash his brain. But, Ravana does not die because of the navel where his life rests. Here, the neck has taken the place of the navel. Now, Balram who is already expert in controlling a man through the neck, his favourite spot, pierces the neck to the extent that his lifeblood spurts resulting in his death. Balram who used to be Hanuman acts like Ravana to kill Rama. It becomes necessary for him to kill Mr Ashok, otherwise he cannot become Rama.

He becomes a murderer after killing his own employer who was his second father. He does not care for the family and becomes responsible for their probable death. He is "a virtual mass murderer" (45) but this murderer becomes a fair man with the name of his master Mr Ashok Sharma in Bangalore. He joins outsourcing which will provide him "real estate, wealth, power, sex" (298). He who used to be "a driver to a master" now becomes "a master of drivers" (302). It was Ravana who kept many gods in his captivity. Here, Balram who is now Mr Ashok Sharma, keeps *Dharam* in his control and makes him a fellow of new generation that knows no moral. In Indian culture, Hanuman is a deity that is always called in adverse circumstances. It is believed that he is *sankatmochan*, one who removes all the troubles in life. Here, Balram Halwai makes his presence available in the hour of crisis. He is a "man people call when they have a crisis" (38). Hanuman loves his tail and it was Ravana who lit his tail that made destruction in Lanka.

Here is Balram Halwai who loves his brain and does not keep anything that may harm it. This is the reason that he does not keep mobile phones because "they corrode a man's brains, shrink his balls, and dry up his semen" and if he loses these things, what will remain in life? Hence, for him his brain which is important for him is the only thing "that a thinking man has in this world" (305). He laughs at the foreigners who go to the Himalayas, or to Benaras, or Bodh Gaya for enlightenment. He suggests them to come to the National Zoo in New Delhi. What can Balram suggest anything more than a zoo? He believes in the philosophy: "Let animals live like animals; let humans live like humans" (276). He is not a human being but a white tiger that will pounce because of his habit of quenching his thirst with the human blood.

Ravana has entered the White Tiger that drinks blood, eats flesh of five-stars girls and roars to make others fear. This tiger knows that everything is for sale. Is the creator of the white tiger for sale? What will be the value of a man who is already sold in the Western market? But, the bottle Johnnie Walker Black has a resale value. Murder and be master. What a message from this new Ramayana, rather Kalyugi Ramayana! How Adiga, the new Valmiki has reversed this Ramayana only to distort the cultural values cherished by every Indian since time immemorial? The poor are the weak and the rich are strong. The strong wipe out the weak and Balram knows that the weak have no right to live. The lamb has no right to live and the tiger must eat it in order to be fat and strong. Bravo Adiga for giving a new message to the world! Evil wins; virtue is defeated. Valmiki's *Ramayana* justifies the victory of good over evil while Adiga's *Ramayana* reverses the script which now can be read as: "Evil always wins over virtue."

Work Cited

Adiga, Aravind. *The White Tiger*. New Delhi: HarperCollins, 2008. **Print.**

5

India Has Never Been Free

> For this land, India has never been free. First the Muslims, then the British bossed us around. In 1947 the British left, but only a moron would think that we became free then. (21-22).

For Adiga, India has got freedom physically but is still slave mentally. The golden bird was caged first by the Muslim rulers who yielded before the British rulers because of their shrewdness in following the principle of divide and rule. In 1947 the British also left India leaving the natives to rule. To think that colonialism is dead is not proper because out of its ashes the ghost of colonialism has appeared to enter the spirit of some monkeys who think themselves the inheritors of the British. The colonial colour is sprinkled over the text of Aravind Adiga's novel *The White Tiger*. The colonial hangover has gone deep in the psyche of the people who think themselves inferior and prove the veracity of the Western concept of the Orient as 'Other'.

Somewhere, Adiga is also a victim of the Western mentality. It is popular about the British that their sun never sets. It became the source of light that enkindles the dark countries through education. The White Man's burden is the burden that is unburdened through providing light—light of knowledge and development. But, under the mask of the white man's burden, the Britishers exploited the resources to the maximum to make themselves rich and powerful. England is an island—the source of power, the water of which becomes light for life-force. Adiga takes the formula of division from England. He divides India into two—the India of Darkness and the India of Light on the basis of ocean and river. For him an ocean is the touchstone for lightness. Wherever the river—the Ganga flows, it makes the area dark and the places that are near the ocean are full of light. Adiga's sick mentality in favour of the British is clear when he says "the ocean brings light to my country". Is he not indicating towards the West, the torch-bearer? Mark the text to show Adiga's illogical division of India on the basis of river and ocean:

> I am talking of a place in India, at least a third of the country, a fertile place, full of rice fields and wheat fields and ponds in the middle of those fields choked with lotuses and water lilies, and water buffaloes wading through the ponds and chewing on the lotuses and lilies. Those who live in this place call it the Darkness. Please understand, Your Excellency, that India is two countries in one: an India of Light, and an India of Darkness. The ocean brings light to my country. Every place on the map of India near the ocean is well-off. But the river brings darkness to India—the black river. (14)

The cowbelt that embraces UP and Bihar is full of darkness because of the black river, i.e. the Ganga. How can the Ganga, a river of illumination, bring darkness to the area is beyond understanding. Only Adiga knows better. The places that are near the 'ocean' are Hyderabad and Bangalore. Bangalore is the only city that is full of light though for him the people who live here are animals. What about Delhi which seems to him crazy? If light means technology, it seems tolerable to some extent. But, now, the technology is embracing every nook and corner connecting not only the Indian villages but also the whole world that has turned into a global village. The light of technology is everywhere. The dark area mentioned by Adiga is actually not as disgusting as he thinks it to be. It is the light of technology that is enkindling the light of America that depends on the Indians. To call the area demarcated by the river Ganga as full of darkness sounds ridiculous.

It is part of the colonial hangover that Indians presume that foreign companies are better and seek their future in them. Slavery has been deep rooted in minds to the extent that Indians today think that the settlement in a foreign country, particularly America, is a sign of progress and an achievement to be proud of. Those who fail to go out of the country work for the foreign companies while living in India. The best example is the field of outsourcing which has most of Indians who basically work for America. It does not matter if India has "no drinking water, electricity, sewage system, public transportation, sense of hygiene, discipline, courtesy, or punctuality" but she has entrepreneurs, especially in the field of technology who have "set up all these outsourcing companies that virtually run America now" (4).

What Adiga says is right. If Indians work for their country, certainly she will progress and become the centre of light for others. There is no sense of relief in thinking that Indians run American companies which are dependent on them. Indians have proved their indispensability to America proving that America depends on Indians and not Indians on America. Such an approach is absurd and cannot change the mentality of slavery. Balram Halwai asks the Chinese Premier not to waste his money on American books because their days are over. He is "tomorrow" the future, while the Americans are "yesterday", the thing of bygone days. He feels that the future lies with the yellow men and the brown men.

Gurgaon is not near the ocean but it is the place where light radiates. It is "the most American part of the city" (121), rather a mini America. Bangalore is the city which is confined to one thing. It is outsourcing which means "doing things in India for Americans over the phone" (298). Are not the Indians slaves to America? It is outsourcing that has tempted Indians because of the matter—the capital that can bring "real estate, wealth, power, sex" (298). Balram Halwai plans to join the outsourcing "one way or the other" even knowing the fact that "men and women in Bangalore live like the animals in a forest do" as they "sleep in the day and then work all night, until two, three, four, five o'clock, depending, because their masters are on the other side of the world, in America" (298). To work for America again shows the colonial influence which has been imprinted on the psyche of Indians who even today think it a matter of pride to work for foreigners.

Aravind Adiga has employed the Black Fort which is a symbol of the colonial hangover. This Black Fort is situated on the "the crest of a hill" which overlooks the village. It is on the hill while the village is in the valley. The contempt for the village is made clear enough to prove the superiority of the English over the native Indians. The fort is not white, rather used by the white, to indicate the domination of the English over Indians. Balram Halwai comes to know about the reality not from his own natives but from the foreign people who tell him "that this fort is as beautiful as anything in Europe" (21). The Black Fort becomes a tool in the hands of the Occident to display his dominance over the Orient. He guesses that this Fort must have been built by "the Turks, or the Afghans, or the English, or whichever foreigner was then ruling India" (21) centuries ago. This is the fort that has been deserted by the foreigner and this indicates the freedom for Indians. Some of the Indians who imitated the English in ways and thinking loved to live here. These Indians are the mimic men better known as monkeys. Hence, now, "a tribe of monkey" (22) occupies the Black Fort. Nobody goes there except a goatherd who takes his flock for grazing. When Balram is a boy, he wishes to enter the Black Fort but his granny Kusum makes him fear with the excuse that "an enormous lizard, the biggest in the whole world" (40) lives in it. He is afraid of lizard which is nothing but a symbol of vice and wickedness. She declares that he is a coward and has no courage, the result of which will be his death if he attempts to enter the Black Fort. But, he makes up his mind to enter the Black Fort to know the mystery behind it. From outside, he has a view of the Black Fort.

> The long loopholes in its wall turned into lines of burning pink at sunrise and burning gold at sunset; the blue sky

> shone through the slits in the stone, while the moon shone on the jagged ramparts, and the monkeys ran wild along the walls, shrieking and attacking each other, as if they were the spirits of the dead warriors reincarnated, refighting their final battles. (40)

The mystery forces him to enter the Black Fort and so he swims and crosses the pond, walks up to the hill and enters it through the door.

What Balram sees there is nothing except "some broken walls and bunch of frightened monkeys" that watch him from a distance. The broken walls are the walls of colonialism and its set tradition while the monkeys are the people who still follow the Western culture and regard the English their master. The entry of Balram makes them afraid of his courage not because he has entered the Black Fort but because of his intention—the intention of being the master, not of being a copycat. He goes higher and higher and from there he looks towards the village which seems to him "little Laxmangarh". He sees the temple, market, sewage, the landlord's mansion and his own house which seems to be the most beautiful sight to him not because it is beautiful as it is not but because of the image of the Orient as exotic, dark and mysterious from the Occidental eyes.

The moment he enters the Fort, he is forced to wear the Western specs which make him see not what he wishes to see but what is being shown to him. The sight prepares the ground for setting his new religion without morality, a market that will make him a white tiger, a neat and clean place where the sewage will not be in view, mansion with light through a chandelier that will frighten the lizards to appear and his identity that will dominate the identity of a water buffalo. When he determines and makes him ready for the action, he does an unusual thing of spitting in the direction of village which represents that he is bidding farewell to the traditional life of the village and embracing the new way of life which is certainly not colonial though touched and inspired by colonialism. He loves his freedom to the extent that he is not ready to become a slave. He recalls the dialogue between God and the Devil and supports the view of the Devil who does not accept the slavery for the sake of heavenly pleasure. Here God is the landlord at the micro level and the British at macro level. It is the Devil who does not accept the dominance of God when he says: "*I am powerful. I am huge. Become my servant again*" (87).

Iqbal's Devil inspires him to become a fierce white tiger without a colonial cage. Even when he is in Bangalore lying under the chandelier, he reminds one of "a black figure in wet khaki uniform who is climbing up the entranceway to a black fort" (87). The black figure is Balram himself. He places his foot "on the ramparts of the Black Fort" where he finds himself surrounded "by a group of amazed monkey" (87).

The monkeys are amazed at the brave deed performed by the white tiger. Others only imitated and remained slaves while the white tiger did the different things and became the master. Again he imagines the scene where God shows "Laxmangarh, its little tributary of the Ganga, and that lies beyond: a million such villages, a billion such people" (87) and interrogates: "*Isn't it all wonderful? Isn't it all grand? Aren't you grateful to be my servant?*" (88). This very interrogation makes the little man angry to the extent that he starts "spitting at God again and again" (88).

God would have created the world in a better way than the present one which has nothing except the inequality of distribution of wealth and the prevalence of social injustice. Balram sees "the black blades of midget fan" slicing the light from the chandelier. Slicing the light by the black blades again represents the rejection of the colonial hangover. Though it is true that Balram does his best to escape from the colonial hangover, even then he becomes its victim as he follows colonialism not word by word but in spirit when he determines to become the boss not only of Bangalore but of the whole world. It is not Balram who is speaking, rather colonialism that makes him claim so.

The English departed for their home. Long live the English! The English left India but left English, the language which became indispensable in day-today life. In spite of the claim for the promotion of the native language, one cannot resist the temptation for the union with it in mind. People say some certain things only in English. Balram does not know how to speak English and supposes the same for the Chinese Premier but even then "there are some things that can be said only in English" (3). He shares with the Chinese Premier that when great people from other countries visit India, the Prime Minister along with their ministers go "to the airport in black cars and get out and do *namastes*" (4) and tell them "how moral and saintly India is" (4). Does one need to say in English that India is saintly and moral? He also tells that under the protocol, the Prime Minister and foreign minister will go to meet him at the airport with garlands and present "home sandalwood statues of Gandhi, and a booklet" (5) that will be "full of information about India's past, present, and future" (5). Actually, Balram thinks that India has nothing to show except Gandhi and India's saintly image. Such are the things that he wishes to say in English, not in the language of the state. Later when he serves the Stork family, he learns many phrases in English. The phrase in English that he learns from Pinky Madam, the ex-wife of his ex-employer Mr Ashok, is, "*What a fucking joke*" (7). Now, Pinky Madam has gone and Balram has taken the place of his master Mr Ashok Sharma. Caliban has learnt now how to curse the master.

Aravind Adiga's *The White Tiger* is an allegory that reveals layers of meanings. Sometimes it is the allegory of colonialism and its repercussions, sometimes the allegory of India's past that has been brutally crushed, and sometimes the allegory of communism that shocks parliamentary form of government. The Stork of Laxmangarh who is not settled in Dhanbad has two sons—Mr Ashok, "the lamb" and Mr Mukesh, "the mongoose".

Mr Ashok goes to America for study and there he marries Pinky Madam who comes to India with the condition that she will return after three months. Mr Ashok is a new coloniser with Pinky Madam. Pinky Madam is the Western culture that has embraced India in the form of Mr Ashok whom she sucks to remove the vital juice of Indian culture. Prospero is now married and comes to his original land to dominate over the black natives. Mr Ashok is the black native made white through the Western cream that Pinky Madam applies on him to make him realise that he is not of his land but of the Western land. Such approach makes him see a different view of India. Luckily the pair gets a new servant Caliban in the form of Balram Halwai who, in spite of being a driver, serves them as a servant performing all the activities. But, this Caliban is not born to be Caliban forever. He is inquisitive and so learns the language of the master though he is mocked by Pinky Madam many times for his dress and mispronunciation of words. When he finds himself fit to be the master, he separates Pinky Madam from Mr Ashok and then kills his master to himself become the master. Caliban has killed Prospero who entered his land not with Miranda but with his wife Pinky Madam. No doubt, he lusts for Pinky Madam like Caliban but does not attempt to rape her as he has learnt to differentiate the valuable things. It is useless to rape for mere lust, rather one should have the power to rape. He has learnt the mantra—the mantra of wealth which provides the power to rape. Hence, he does not hesitate when Pinky Madam asks him to drive her at night to the airport.

Balram is now free to tempt Mr Ashok to come in the net and later everything what he plans happens. Now, Caliban disguises himself as Mr Ashok Sharma after killing him, and with his money settles down in Bangalore in order to become the white tiger, the boss who will dominate the world through his entrepreneurship. This Caliban who was exploited now has learnt to exploit others. No doubt, colonialism is over in name but in practical life it is still present in the mind that knows no sentiments. Where is the victory of Balram Halwai who has worn the dress of Ashok Sharma, the capitalist, and this dress makes him kick his employees as soon as they complete their work?

Balram Halwai is indebted to his master because of many things that he has learnt from him. He used to hear the chatting of Mr Ashok and Pinky Madam about "life, about India, about America—and a bit of English too" (47). His best ideas are not his but are borrowed from his master Mr Ahsok, Mr Mukesh and also others. He confesses that he is not "an original thinker" but "an original *listener*" (47). Caliban has not thought anything original, rather listened to their masters' thoughts. What he has done something new is that he translated them into reality. They speak theory but he is practical. Later, when he becomes the boss in Bangalore, he sends Dharam to the English school so that he may not suffer from inferiority complex. He feels happy when Dharam pronounces "English like a rich man's son" and knows how to say "pizza the way Mr Ashok" uttered. Balram never learns these things but makes his nephew Dharam learn the way of the English man. Does he not colonise the mind of Dharam in favour of the white man or is he replying to the white men that a black man can also perform what they can? Balram himself is half-baked because of the bonded labour that made him devoid of education. He is a man who can "read and write" but does not know "what he's read" and this makes Mr Ashok declare that he is "half-baked" and "the country is full of people like him" (10). Indian Parliamentary democracy is the machine that produces half-baked characters like Balram and here lies the tragedy of this country. Mark below Balram Halwai's generalisation of the tragedy of the country that produces half-baked people:

> Me, and thousands of others in this country like me, are half-baked, because we were never allowed to complete our schooling. Open our skulls, look in with a penlight, and you'll find an odd museum of ideas: sentences of history or mathematics remembered from school textbooks (no boy remembers his schooling like one who was taken out of school, let me assure you), sentences about politics read in a newspaper while waiting for someone to come to an office, triangles and pyramids seen on the torn pages of the old geometry textbooks which every tea shop in this

> country uses to wrap its snacks in, bits of All India Radio news bulletins, things that drop into your mind, like lizards from the ceiling, in the half-hour before falling asleep—all these ideas, half formed and half digested and half correct, mix up with other half-cooked ideas in your head, and I guess these half-formed ideas bugger one another, and make more half-formed ideas, and this is what you act on and live with. (10-11)

No doubt, it is a tragedy with the country but the bigger tragedy is that those who are full-baked become the servant of those who are half-baked. Balram believes that "Entrepreneurs are made from half-baked clay" (11) but the full-baked people complete their school and university education but in the end, "wear nice suits, join companies, and take orders from other men for the rest of their lives" (11). His father who pulled rickshaw wishes an education for his son so that he may not be "a human beast of burden" (27) and live like a man. In school, he gets the title of the white tiger from the school inspector who regards him as "an intelligent, honest, vivacious fellow in this crowd of thugs and idiots" (35). He is really a white tiger that comes once in a generation.

What is done by Balram is not expected from an ordinary man. He is a man who has a dream—a dream of seeing what is beautiful in the word. He believes in what Iqbal utters: "*They remain slaves because they can't see what is beautiful in this world*" (40). He is not born to be a slave. He learns about politics, coal and China in the Stork family. Whatever he hears he absorbs and later in life gives them a practical shape. In Delhi, he sees the apartment blocks "all shiny and new, and with nice big English names" (128) like Buckingham Towers B Block, etc. Even Indians have not come out from slavery, and show their respect to the erstwhile boss by giving English names to the streets and buildings.

Balram Halwai does not forget the day when Mr Ashok asks him to wear the dress of the Indian Maharaja and offer the dishes to Pinky Madam on her birthday. The scene reminds one of the birthday of the Queen and the celebration thereafter in the colonised countries. Outwardly, what Mr Mukesh does is just to please Pinky Madam but actually it is an insult to the traditional Indian values. An Indian Maharaja is made to serve Pinky Madam from America.

> On her birthday, for instance, he had me dress up as a maharaja, with a red turban and dark cooling glasses, and serve them their food in this costume. I'm not talking of any ordinary home cooking, either—he got me to serve her some of that stinking stuff that comes in cardboard boxes and drives all the rich absolutely crazy.
>
> She laughed and laughed and laughed when she saw me in my costume, bowing low to her with the cardboard box. I served them, and then, as Mr Ashok had instructed, stood near the portrait of Cuddles and Puddles with folded hands and waited.
>
> 'Ashok,' she said. 'Now hear this. Balram, what is it we're eating?'
>
> I knew it was a trap, but what could I do?—I answered. The two of them burst into giggles.
>
> 'Say it again, Balram.'
>
> They laughed again.
>
> 'It's not piJJa. It's pizza. Say it properly.'
>
> 'Wait—you're mispronouncing it too. There's a *T* in the middle. *Peet. Zah.*' (154)

Balram Halwai in the dress of Maharaja is the symbol of India who is colonised and made 'others' in the view of the West. The red turban and dark cooling glasses make him ridiculous. He is asked to serve the Western food pizza in a cardboard box. He stands near her bowing his head to her who laughs at him in this costume. More insultingly the Westernised Mr Ashok makes the Caliban Balram stand near the portraits of the puppies with folded hands. This is an extreme insult not only to Balram but also the Indian Maharaja who is made the target of fun to display the image of India as other. Pinky Madam is not satisfied with it and so she asks him to name the food that they are eating only to make him realise his low status as a man who cannot pronounce a word like pizza. Both Mr Ashok, the Westernised mixed breed, and Pinky Madam laugh at the embarrassing mental state of Balram who remains helpless. After this, both go for a drive and in her drunkard state, she asks Balram, who is in the Indian Maharaja's dress to get down. She returns again and asks him if he is angry with her and thinks that she has left him. He does not react to it, rather very calmly replies: "Employers are like mother and father. How can one be angry with them" (162)? But, later, when he is free from duty, he takes the car out of the apartment, dresses like a maharaja and goes without any purpose. He drives the car around the malls, hoots at the girls, plays on his music, runs A/C at full speed, returns and finally takes the car into the garage. There he does one thing; he spits over the seats and then wipes them clean. This is the anger that he releases by taking the car and becoming the real maharaja. His spitting over the seats shows his hatred for Mr Ashok and Pinky Madam who insulted him. When he murders his master and becomes a rich man, he thinks of selling everything so that he may "start a school—an English-language school—for poor children in Bangalore" (321). This is the school where "the facts of the life" will be taught. This school will be "full of white tigers, unleashed on Bangalore" and with their help he will become "the Boss of Bangalore" (321). Caliban decides to make more Calibans in order to oppose Prosperos and their white beauties. The white tigers have learnt English language not as a part of slavery but as a part of reaction to abuse the West in the same language. He says all this and thinks that it is "worthwhile to know, just for a day, just for an hour, just for a *minute*, what it means not to be a servant" (321). But, to forget the torture, oppression and exploitation forever is impossible. Somewhere in any corner the remembrance of colonialism is ever present. Besides, is there any guarantee that Balram Halwai, the white tiger, will not repeat the history of the English after getting power?

It is woman who suffered the worst from colonisers who exploited her to the maximum physically and psychologically.

She was twice colonised—first by the colonisers and then by her own native people who exploited her not less than the colonisers. Today she is being exploited in the name of consumerism—a part of globalisation that has turned her into a commodity that has its value in rupees. Adiga has shown in *The White Tiger* that a woman is for sale. Every woman has her price.

When Balram completes the course of driving, the old driver appreciates his skill in learning, calling him "a surprise package" (57) and thinks of a reward for him. The reward is that he takes him to the area where prostitution is operated. When Balram walks the area, he is wonderstruck at "the gorgeous women" who jeer and taunt him "from behind their grilled windows" (58) with the request of having sex with them. Mark the excerpt for the commodification of the woman's body:

> The old driver explained the nature of the wares on offer. Up in one building, sting on a windowsill in such a way that we could see the full spread of their gleaming dark legs, were the 'Americans': girls in short skirts and high platform shoes, carrying pink handbags with names in English written on them in sequins. They were slim and athletic—for men who like the Western kind. In this corner, sitting in the threshold of an open house, the 'traditionals' –fat, chunky types in saris, for those who like value for their money. There were eunuchs in one window—teenagers in the next window. The face of a small boy appeared from between a woman's legs and then vanished.
>
> A blinding flash of light: a blue door opened, and four light-skinned Nepali women, in gorgeous red petticoats, look out.
>
> 'Them!' I shouted. 'Them! Them! Them!'
>
> 'Good,' the old driver said. 'I like that too—I always go for the foreign ones.' (58)

Woman is not a woman or a human being but a ware or a product on sale. Balram loves the light-skinned Nepali woman with the red petticoat with whom he enjoys sex. It is surprising that the old driver also loves to have sex with the foreign women. Temptation towards the white skin shows the mental slavery of Indians who still care for the white skin. The white skin has become a craze among the Indians to the extent that the creams that make fair are sold in the markets. Even Balram whose face is blackish is of "half a mind to try one of those skin-whitener creams they've launched these days so Indian men can look white as Westerners" (12). He neither rejects the charm of white skin nor accepts it completely. Though in the end, he makes his intention clear that "all the skin-whitening creams sold in the markets of India" (318) will not clean his hands that have murdered his master.

Pinky Madam who is an individual with an identity of her own cannot be chained to the masculine cage. Others want to conceal the case of hit-and-run while Pinky Madam, "the lady with short skirts" somehow, becomes a lady "with a conscience" (180). She wishes to find the family of the hit child so that she may offer compensation. But, this very attitude makes the Stork say that "she has gone crazy" and rebukes his son Mr Ashok for not controlling his wife the way they used to do in the village. Such attitude reflects the colonised way of treating the woman. White skin with golden hair becomes the craze for Balram Halwai. Mark the excerpt for the woman's saleability:

> 'I don't care. She just has to have golden hair—like in the shampoo advertisements.'
>
> 'Cheapest is ten, twelve thousand.'
>
> 'That's too much. He won't pay more than four thousand seven hundred.'
>
> 'Six thousand five hundred, Country-Mouse. That's the minimum. White skin has to be respected.' (228)

But, when he finds the girl with golden hair a fake because of the dye job, he shouts at the manager "pulling the girl by hair" which is "not real gold". The manager speaks in the same way making Balram realise that what he will have for seven thousand. The real girl with golden hair costs forty or fifty thousand. This is the way that women are treated as commodities which are open for bargain. When he becomes the boss in Bangalore with a lot of money, he does not go to the red light areas where poor women live "in bird cages and get treated like animals" (304) but likes to buy girls in the five-star hotels. Now, he does not run after the golden-coloured hair which has made him sick. He shares his experience of sex with girls and declares first that "Indians girls are the best" (304) but later improvises his statement calling them "second-best". The Nepali girls attract him more than the Indian girls.

Are women in India free when they are treated like animals? When they are turned into the objects for sale, they are purchased and exploited fully. Where is freedom? India is still a slave country where women who were earlier respected now become a victim of colonisation that out of globalisation has shown them a path that leads to their slavery. Pinky wishes to go back to America as per the promise but Mr Ashok does not wish to return now to New York as he finds better chances and amenities in India. He convinces her saying that "things have changed so much in India. There are so many more things I could do here than in New York now" (89) and also makes her believe that "The way things are changing in India now, this place is going to be like America in ten years" (89). It seems that he can have more control over Pinky Madam in India than in New York where she feels more comfortable than in India. He imagines that he can colonise her in India but she has her own identity and is not a woman to be chained. She returns to New York when she realises that Mr Ashok here has got what he could not get in New York. He has power to rule over the servants who are not better than his people. He tells Pinky Madam why he does not wish to return to New York.

> Plus, I like it better here. We've got people to take care of us here—our drivers, our watchmen, our masseurs. Where in New York will you find someone to bring you tea and sweet biscuits while you're still lying in bed, the way Ram Bahadur does for us? You know, he's been in my family for thirty years—we call him a servant, but he's part of the family. (89)

With the Western mindset, he finds the way to colonise the people though in a modest manner. He exploits them with love and care.

Colonial hangover is also noticeable even in the liquor that is also categorised into English liquor and Indian liquor. Indians have a liking for English liquor because it is a drink from the English men who got success after success and enjoyed life with this drink. The name of the shop where Balram and Ram Persad go to take bottle for their master is "JACKPOT' ENGLISH LIQUOR SHOP INDIAN-MADE FOREIGN LIQUOR SOLD HERE" (72). It is in India that foreign liquor is made and sold. The foreign liquor has hypnotised the Indian mind with the superiority over the Indian liquor.

Men are also categorised as "Indian liquor men" and "English liquor men". Indian liquor is meant for villagers while English liquor for the rich. The price list is also displayed at the shop. Black Dog is the whisky that belongs to the first class category worth rupees 1330 per bottle. Ram Persad asks for a full bottle of Black Dog. It is the "first name in the first class category of whisky" which is taken by the Stork and his sons. Balram's eyes are "dazzled by the sight of so much English liquor" (75). The first class whisky is Black Dog, the name of which reveals the colonial treatment from the English. Dog is considered to be faithful and placing 'black' before 'dog' somewhere has the link with the Indians. Balram, no doubt, shows his longing for the whisky but later on uses Johnnie Walker Black, the bottle with resale value. He hits the bottle three times "into the crown of his skull, smashing through to his brains" (285). The use of the bottle for killing his master makes him free from slavery. He uses the English bottle to kill the Westernised master.

White, the colour which is associated with the British reflects power and source of light for others. Balram Halwai sees the rich people in the white T-shirt. He buys a T-shirt which was "white, with a small word in English in the centre" (150) and also wishes for the black shoes. The white T-shirt and black shoes will help him to enter the mall. When he kills his master, he picks up the bundle that has the white cotton T-shirt with lots of white space and one word in English. He changes his clothes and wears the white T-shirt. This T-shirt brings power to him and makes him the source of light for the people of Bangalore. As he is a lover of freedom, he loves China because it did not let the British dominate. He infers that "the future of the world lies with the yellow man and the brown man" (6). The day of the British has come to an end and the reason is that "the white skin man has wasted himself through buggery, mobile phone usage, and drug abuse" (6). The wearing of the white T-shirt with a letter in English still reflects the colonial hangover. But, with the passage of time, he realises that the storehouse of power has shifted to China.

It seems absurd that Adiga makes his protagonist say: "One fact about India is that you can take almost anything you hear about the country from the prime minister and turn it upside down and then you will have the truth about that thing" (15). What a logic Adiga gives here! Is it so that what is said about India by Indians is not true? Does the Prime Minister of India tell a lie? Why does he do so? Is there any need to turn the statements upside down to know the truth? Adiga also thinks that Indians cannot be free because of religion that teaches them to be servants throughout life. He divides the deity on the basis of darkness and light. The people of darkness worship Hanuman who is the perfect instance of devotion and service. Hence, Balram Halwai thinks that it is hard "for a man to win his freedom in India" (19).

The landlords who exploit the poor people are the colonialists in disguise. India became free but still today the landlords rule over the people who feel helpless and have no courage to go against them. In *The White Tiger*, four landlords namely, Buffalo, Stork, Wild Boar and Raven, rule over the villages though they have their sons and daughters settled in the cities because of the fear of the Naxals. The Stork who has a river in his share takes a cut of every catch of fish caught in the river and a toll from every boatman. The Wild Boar who is the owner of the agriculture land gives work only to those who not only bow down before him but also agree to give a part of their wages. The Raven who is in possession of the grazing area takes a cut from the goatherds and if they fail to give a cut he likes to dip his beak into their backsides. The Buffalo takes money from the users of the road. The four landlords are no better than colonialists in putting the natives under their control for exploitation. Balram Halwai holds the *varna* system responsible for the colonial cage that does not let the people come out of it:

> See, this country, in its days of greatness, when it was the richest nation on earth, was like a zoo. A clean, well-kept, orderly zoo. Everyone in his place, everyone happy. Goldsmiths here Cowherds here. Landlords there. The man called a Halwai made sweets.The man called a cowherd tended cows. The untouchable cleaned faeces. Landlords were kind to their serfs. Women covered their heads with a veil and turned their eyes to the ground when talking to strange men. (63)

But, when India got freedom, the cages of the ancient days had been let open. The animals came out and attacked one another. The attack resulted in two castes—"Men with Big Bellies and Men with Small Bellies" which set the two destines accordingly either "eat or eaten up" (64). This is the new kind of colonialism. One who is mighty will rule over the weak. Even the democratic system also favours the strong. It is the democratic system that makes the landlord Stork bow down before Vijay, the pigherd's son. The Great Socialist feels pleasure in teasing the Stork and his sons. The British freed India but left the politicians behind them as their successors. Politicians know only one language—the language of exploitation in any form.

Adiga has used the metaphor of rooster coop which also prepares a colonial cage for the people who naturally become a victim without realising that they are caught. Balram is asked to sign an affidavit that makes him take the responsibility of the case of hit-and-run on his shoulder. He signs it and does not think of running away or speaking the truth to the judge that he has not committed the crime. India is free but Indians are still slaves—slaves to the coop. A few people who own capital rule over so many poor people. A person of pervert nature can come out of the coop. As Balram Halwai is a man of pervert nature, he does not care for his family. He remains silent for the time being in the hope of a better opportunity. He tolerates the insult from the hands of Mr Ashok and Pinky Madam who make him realise that he is still uncivilised as he scratches his groin and does not know how to brush his teeth to keep them clean. It is the West that presents the East as 'other' making him feel why it is other. Balram cries: "Why had my father never told me not to scratch my groin? Why had my father never taught me to brush my teeth in milky foam? Why had he raised me to live like an animal? Why do all the poor live amid such filth, such ugliness?" but these cries remain confined to him because in spite of his longing for brushing and spitting, he cannot "spit his past out so easily" (151). He becomes so angry within that he embraces even the vices of his master and later even murders him to take his place. He changes his fortune from "a driver to a master" to "a master of drivers" (302). He does not expect the freedom for the Indians who wait "for the war of their freedom to come from somewhere else—from the jungles, from the mountains, from China, from Pakistan. That will never happen. Every man must make his own Benaras" (304).

Balram thinks that Indians will be slaves because instead of reading the book of revolution that sits in belly, they like to sit "in front of colour TVs and watching cricket and shampoo advertisements" (304). Hence, freedom of India is a hopeless case. He is sure of one thing—that the white men will come to an end in his lifespan. The place of white men will be taken by the yellow men and brown men.

Balram Halwai is now a man who has established his identity. It does not matter to him that he had to murder his master. In this country, he shares with the Chinese Premier: "Kill enough people and they will put up bronze statues to you near Parliament House in Delhi" (318). He feels that "the moment you recognise what is beautiful in this world, you stop being a slave" (276) and he recommends that "if you taught every poor boy how to paint, that would be the end of the rich in India" (276). The need is to know the value of freedom but the problem with the Indians is that "free people don't know the value of freedom" (117).

No doubt, India is free now; she is free geographically but her people are still in the chains. The saying: "India is a free country with slave people" is as true as the saying "India is a rich country with poor people" is. Slavery or freedom is not a matter of geography, rather it is mental affair. That's why Adiga's Balram cares for his brain which is the only thing that "a thinking man has in this world" (305).

Work Cited

Adiga, Aravind. *Th. White Tiger*. New Delhi: HarperCollins, 2008. **Print**.

6

This Fucked-up System Called Parliamentary Democracy

Democracy, a household word, is derived from two Greek words—*demos* and *kratos*—that with the meaning 'people' and 'power ' respectively connote 'the power of the people'. Though "a degenerate or perverted form of constitutional government" for Aristotle (*Political Theory* 451), it is still the best form of government that ensures people's participation directly or indirectly in exercising political control over state affairs. Nothing is final because of the continuation of the process of learning. "All government", C.D. Burns writes, "is a method of education, but the best education is self-education; therefore the best government is self-government which is democracy" (*Political Theory* 450).

In spite of some hindrances like regionalism, casteism, illiteracy, poverty, laziness and communalism etc. that mar the progress, it is the government, to use Lincoln's words, "of the people, by the people, and for the people" (*Political Theory* 447). It is the form of government that represents public opinion while upholding the individual liberty. It provides a school of citizenship for the people who acquire political education, embrace patriotism, and learn how to bring order and progress in the society without neglecting moral virtues. No doubt, this form of government embraces the social justice as a philosophy harmonising liberty and equality for the sustainable development but there are some certain flaws that have fractured its structure. More emphasis on quantity than quality, bossism, slow working, expensiveness, dominance of the local mafias, frequent election, failures of coalition governments, dictatorship of the majority are some of the viruses that have entered its body and made it weak from inside.

After independence, India has embraced the parliamentary form of government. She has the credit of being the largest democracy in the world in spite of some certain defects that have crept into it. The Indian democratic system does its best to ensure the representation of the will of people through the Constitution. It provides the maximum opportunities to the people for exercising the freedom of self-determination with moral obligation. No one can deny the fact of criminalisation of politics in recent years. The white cover of the Indian democratic system has become black because of the dirt in the form of unemployment, the gulf between the rich and the poor, bribery, corruption, hunger, starvation and illiteracy. But, it does not mean that the democratic system is responsible for all these monsters. The need is not to make an end but to amend to have a better result. Ashirvatham writes: "If democracy is a bad form of government, we are justified in asking, what is the way out? Is there any other form of government which is as good as democracy, if not better" (*Political Theory* 454)?

Aravind Adiga's *The White Tiger* offers a commentary on the drawbacks of democracy. The protagonist Balram Halwai seems to be the mouthpiece of Adiga, a Marxist, as he has highlighted the dark side of democracy in such an exaggerated way that it seems that India is not a country worth living because of the corrupted political system. He holds parliamentary democracy responsible for India's backwardness. He states: "There's only one thing wrong with this place—we have this fucked-up system called parliamentary democracy. Otherwise, we'd be just like China" (*The White Tiger* 156). India has embraced democracy as a political system only in name, not in the real sense. What is noted in India is the mockery of Democracy. Ironically he writes to the Chinese Premier:

> O, democracy!
>
> Now, Mr. Premier, the little take-home pamphlet that you will be given by the prime minister will no doubt contain a very large section on the splendor of democracy in India—the awe-inspiring spectacle of one billion people casting their votes to determine their own future, in full freedom of franchise, and so on and so forth.
>
> I gather you yellow-skinned men, despite your triumphs in sewage, drinking water, and Olympic gold medals, still don't have democracy. Some politician on the radio was saying that that's why we Indians are going to bet you: we may not have sewage, drinking water, and Olympic gold medals, but we do have democracy.
>
> If I were making a country, I'd get the sewage pipes first, then the democracy, then I'd go about giving pamphlets and statues of Gandhi to other people, but what do I know? I'm just a murderer!
>
> (*The White Tiger* 95-96)

India is proud of having the largest democracy in the world. It doesn't matter if she has not provided the basic necessities to her people. Giving the basic amenities to every citizen is the first priority of any political system. What Adiga's protagonist observes is that India has democracy in form, not in spirit. The failure of the social justice to every individual speaks the story of the failure of the democratic system. The grand show of the billions of the people casting their votes seems to be a success of democracy. But, in reality, they do not have the right to determine their future because of certain circumstances which make them dwarfs or helpless against the muscle power. China has got success in providing the basic amenities to her citizens without having a democratic system. India may beat China not in basic amenities but in having democracy. Democracy becomes the icon of India's success. Balram admits that he is a murderer and has no right to say or offer anything for the betterment of the country but if he is given a chance to shape India's fate, he will make the sewage pipes available first, then he will think of democracy. He mocks at the democratic system that has not yet provided the sewage pipes resulting in the filthy Indian scenario. In India, democracy has failed because of its inability in following the ideals on the ground level. It has become responsible for poverty, unemployment and exploitation.

The success of any democratic system depends on the honest and able politicians but it is generally seen that those who are dishonest, corrupt and less educated win the elections by virtue of muscle power and become policy makers. The intelligent, honest and highly educated get defeated and remain helpless because of the criminalisation of politics. Ashirvatham writes: "Power in a democracy falls into the hands of the demagogue, the grafter, and the boss. Leaders of first-rate ability are not chosen. People are jealous of superiority. Therefore, they choose popular men rather than able men to lead them" (*Political Theory* 451). The protagonist thinks that "Entrepreneurs are made from half-baked clay" (*The White Tiger* 11) while those who are fully formed "after twelve years of school and three years of university, wear nice suits, join companies, and take orders from other men for the rest of their lives" (*The White Tiger* 11). Rulers are half-baked while the ruled are full-baked. Better to be half-baked like Balram Halwai to rule over the people. Better to rule than to serve. He calls his life story "the Autobiography of a Half-Baked Indian" (*The White Tiger* 11). This is India where the mediocre rules over the talent. Talent becomes a dwarf before the mediocre with guts. If the half-baked man has no guts and no desire to rise, he will remain half-baked throughout life. A democratic country is expected to provide education to all the citizens. Compulsory primary education to all children is now the basic need of any country.

It seems that this country is the factory that produced half-baked Indians more in number than the full-baked ones. The more corrupt a politician is the more chances he has to win. The Great Socialist is an instance of corruption in politics. Criminalisation of politics has become the golden rule in this country. He cites the cases of politicians who indulged in criminal cases:

> You see, a total of ninety-three criminal cases—for murder, rape, grand larceny, gun-smuggling, pimping, and many other such minor offences—are pending against the Great Socialist and his ministers at the present moment. Not easy to get convictions when the judges are judging in Darkness, yet three convictions have been delivered, and three of the ministers are currently in jail, but continue to be ministers. The Great Socialist himself is said to have embezzled one billion rupees from the Darkness, and transferred that money into a bank account in a small, beautiful country in Europe full of white people and black money.
>
> (*The White Tiger* 97-98)

What future will be of the country where criminals rule and form policy? Ministers, in spite of being in jail, continue to be ministers. It is a fact that one who gets money by hook or crook deposits his black money in a foreign country. These corrupt politicians have their account in Switzerland where they have deposited Indian money. These corrupt politicians have blocked the Indian money which can be used for various projects to bring prosperity to Indian people. Politics has become a profession. One who has guts along with the muscles and money can try to become the boss. Vijay, the bus-conductor from Laxmangarh, is the ideal hero of Balram Halwai. He changes his professions from time to time. This happens only in a democratic country like India that the Stork (the landlord) has to bow down before the mediocre Vijay. Ironically he says: "I waited by the gate and watched. The Stork himself came out to see Vijay, and bowed down before him—a landlord bowing before a pigherd's son! The marvels of democracy" (*The White Tiger* 103)! The winning politicians do not forget to torture and exploit their adversaries. They do their best in taking revenge upon the landlords who earlier exploited them. Here is an excerpt that reflects the mental attitude of the politician and the mindset of the people who voted for him only because the Great Socialist used to insult the landlords. The Great Socialist asks the Mongoose to hold the spittoon for him in order to humiliate him.

> When I came back with the spittoon, he coolly turned to the Mongoose and said, 'Son, won't you hold the spittoon for me?'
>
> The Mongoose refused to move, so that Great Socialist took the spittoon from my hands and held it out.
>
> 'Take it, son.'
>
> The Mongoose took it.
>
> Then the Great Socialist spat into the spittoon, three times.
>
> The Mongoose's hands trembled; his face turned black with shame.
>
> 'Thank you for that, son,' the Great Socialist said, wiping his lips. He turned to me and tickled his forehead. 'Where was I, now?'
>
> There you have it. That was the positive side of the Great Socialist. He humiliated all our masters—that's why we kept voting him back in.
>
> (*The White Tiger* 105)

It is surprising that people vote for the Great Socialist not because of his ability or any good quality but because of his habit of humiliating the masters. The servants take pleasures and feel satisfied when they see their masters being humiliated. They do not have courage to retaliate against their masters and so, when they see someone humiliating them, they feel their selves revenging upon them.

In India, no government is stable, the result of which is frequent election. Election is not a means of political education to the people, rather it has turned into a disease. Balram Halwai considers it the worst disease. He shares this with the Chinese Premier: "These are the three main diseases of this country, sir: typhoid, cholera, and election fever. This last one is the worst; it makes people talk and talk about things that they have no say in" (*The White Tiger* 98). Election is the disease that makes people talk and talk but their discussions remain useless. The voters discuss the election in the Laxmangarh "like eunuchs discussing the Kama Sutra"

(*The White Tiger* 98). They have been given the voting rights but they are used by others through booth capturing, etc. Hence, they remain eunuchs and their discussion is just like the discussion on the *Kamasutra*. The age of voting right is eighteen and, hence, the officer who has come for registering voters considers Balram eighteen years as eligible for the voting rights. This is not only with Balram but all the working boys at the tea-shop. Mark the excerpt for the ridiculous way for enrolling the new voters:

> A man in a government uniform sat at the teacher's desk in the schoolroom, with a long book and a black pen, and he was asking everyone two questions.
>
> 'Name.'
>
> 'Balram Halwai.'
>
> 'Age.'
>
> 'No age.'
>
> 'No date of birth?'
>
> 'No, sir, my parents didn't make note of it.'
>
> He looked at me and said, 'I think you're eighteen. I think you turned eighteen today. You just forgot, didn't you?'
>
> I bowed to him. 'That's correct, sir. I forgot. It was my birthday today.'
>
> 'Good boy.'
>
> And then he wrote that down in his book and told me to go away. So I got a birthday from the government.
>
> I had to be eighteen. All of us in the tea shop had to be eighteen, the legal age to vote. There was an election coming up, and the tea shop owner had already sold us.
>
> (*The White Tiger* 96-97)

Adiga through his protagonist mocks at the system which, in spite of being ideal is not ideal on the practical ground. On the surface, anyone who is eighteen years old has the right to vote but actually has no say in the plan. Hence, democracy becomes opposed to liberty in spite of being in favour of equality and liberty. It gives more importance to quantity rather than to quality. Votes are counted, not the quality of the persons who voted. Judgement based on expert knowledge is thrown into the dustbin. It is the crowd, not the rational people, that determines the fate of the candidates. Slogans like "Rise against the rich! Support the great Socialist. Keep the landlords out!" (*The White Tiger* 91) set the tone of the election time. The four Animals (landlords) also form a party "All India Social Progressive Front" in opposition to the Great Socialist.

Illegal practices are adopted by the politicians for winning the election. Generally it is seen that the ruling party misuses the media and government machinery in its favour. But, thanks to the Election Commission that it has curbed the political parties and put the limitations on the candidates in the form of some strict rules. Even then, malpractices are being practised. Booth capturing is one such practice practised by the candidates by virtue of their muscle power. It is surprising that everyone votes for the Great Socialist in the election. How is it possible that all the voters voted for him? "They had counted 2,341 votes in that booth. Everyone had voted for the Great Socialist" (*The White Tiger* 101). The protagonist murders his masters, runs away and finally settles down in Bangalore. He satirizes on the Indian voting system. No doubt, the voting right is a pious right but it is never used by the person who has it. Mark the ironical way of the protagonist to point out the fake voting often done on the booth under the influence of the muscle power.

> Here's a little souvenir of your Indian visit to keep with you. Balram Halwai is a vanished man, a fugitive, someone whose whereabouts are unknown to the police, right?
>
> Ha!
>
> The police know exactly where to find me. They will find me dutifully voting on election day at the voting booth in the school compound in Laxmangarh in Gaya District, as I have done in every general, state, and local election since I turned eighteen.

> I am India's most faithful voter, and I still have not seen the inside of a voting booth.
>
> (*The White Tiger* 102)

Balram Halwai satirizes on the way the elections are held in India. He is a banished man because of the murder that he has committed. Though he is wanted by the police, he uses his voting right in every election—be it local or state or general without going inside the booth. What he wishes to say is that his voting right is used by someone else. Fake voting cases in India are not new. "Election can be managed in India; it's not like in America" (*The White Tiger* 213). But, sometimes, the result surprises the people. It happens with Mr. Ashok and Mr. Mukesh who are sure of the victory of the ruling party but on the contrary the Great Socialist wins. They favour the candidates in order to get out of the income tax mess. After winning the elections, politicians do not do anything for the country; rather they are interested either in making money or in humiliating the opposition. They are expected to be treated obsequiously. How intelligently he recognises the two people as politicians! "The two men slapped him on the back; he bowed, and opened the doors for them himself. If he was kissing arse like this, they had to be politicians" (*The White Tiger* 270). These two politicians are sadists as they wish to see the rich men in trouble. It gives them more pleasure than the pleasure of erection. "Are you sure? I'd love to send some boys over. I just love to see a rich man righted up. It's better than an erection" (*The White Tiger* 271). One of the politicians regards the people of South as *negroes* and considers himself the son of Aryans. Mark the excerpt for the hoax that becomes clear from the conversation between the two politicians on the issue of victory in South:

> 'You know what the best part of this election is?
>
> 'What?'
>
> 'The way we've spread down south. We've got a foot-hold in Bangalore too. And you know that's where the future is.'

> 'The south? Bullshit.'
>
> 'Why not? One in every three new office buildings in India is being built in Bangalore. It *is* the future.'
>
> '*Fuck* all that. I don't believe a word. The south is full of Tamils. You know who the Tamils are? *Negroes*. We're the sons of the Aryans who came to India. We made them our slaves. And now they give us lectures. *Negroes*.'
>
> (*The White Tiger* 272)

The ideal of democracy is justice from every angle but it is more abused than used for social welfare. Corruption has embraced it and injected bribery in its veins. It is crying and voicing the common people but its voice is silenced because of the money power, the magic of which enwraps electors, politicians, bureaucrats and judges. The people now have two castes—"Men with Big Bellies, and Men with Small Bellies" (*The White Tiger* 64). Caste does not count. What counts is the size of the belly. Hence, here are only two destinies "eat—or get eaten up" (*The White Tiger* 64). The problem with this country is that "Free people don't know the value of freedom" (*The White Tiger* 117) and love to remain in the dark. Why do the people not keep themselves in the light like him and use chandeliers all the time?

It is difficult to locate responsibility under the democratic system. One holds the other responsible for the drawbacks. Government makes the schemes for the welfare of the people. It is doubtful whether such schemes are properly executed or not. Grants worth crores are given for the development of the villages. But, nothing changes except the politicians' bellies that grow larger than ever. Here is an excerpt that reflects the condition of the village in spite of the grant provided for its development.

> Electricity poles—defunct
>
> Water tap—broken
>
> Children—too lean and short for their age, and with over-sized heads from which vivid eyes shine, like the guilty conscience of the government of India.

> Yes, a typical Indian village paradise, Mr Jiabao.
> (*The White Tiger* 20)

On paper, it is the ideal village with all the facilities. Electricity and water pipes are in the paper. Children are not underfed according to the health norms. But, the reality is not what the paper says. The protagonist has used the phrase "guilty conscience of the government of India" knowingly because the government knows the reality but remains helpless because of the corrupt inoperative system that has made it lame. This corruption has entered even in the temple of education. The teacher steals the money of the government scheme of providing *roti* and *dal* to each student on the plea that he has not got his salary for a long time. Even the people know it but do not blame the teacher. How can one expect "a man in a dung heap to smell sweet" (*The White Tiger* 33)? What Adiga wishes to show is that in India teachers are either underpaid or not paid salary in time. Government schemes become a mockery in such a democratic system. Not to talk of educational institutions, even in the hospital, the ward boy gives the information about the doctor when he is given a ten-rupee note by the protagonist. The Great Socialist makes an open auction of the vacant post lying in the hospital. "Now, each time this post falls vacant, the Great Socialist lets all the big doctors know that he's having an open auction for that post. The going rate for this post is about four hundred thousand rupees these days" (*The White Tiger* 49). What will be the future of such a country where doctors are appointed not by virtue of their qualification? If one-third salary is given to the Great Socialist as bribery, he allows the doctor Ram Pandey to work in some private hospital. Mark the excerpt for the glaring instance of the bribery in the hospital:

> 'Now, you—Dr Ram Pandey—will kindly put one-third of your salary in my palm. Good boy. In return, I do *this*.' He made a tick on the imaginary ledger. 'You can keep the rest of your government salary and go work in some private hospital for the rest of the week. Forget the village.

> Because according to this ledger you've *been* there. You've *treated* my wounded leg. You've *healed* that girl's jaundice.' (*The White Tiger* 50)

There is no end of bribery in India under this democratic system. The Government officials have the stature or pictures of Gandhi but are more interested not in the ideals of Gandhi but in Gandhi on the notes. Mr. Ashok is fed up with the political system in India. He states: "We're driving past Gandhi, after just having given a bribe to a minister. It's a *fucking joke*, isn't it" (*The White Tiger* 137). Not to talk of the politicians, everybody indulges in bribery. When Balram has settled in Bangalore he continues to give bribery to the police. He says: "There is no end of things in India, Mr Jiabao, as Mr Ashok so correctly used to say. You'll have to keep paying and paying the fuckers. But I complain about the police the way the rich complain; not the way the poor complain" (*The White Tiger* 310). With the help of bribery, one can come out of the mess. In India, there is a way to come out of the mess. The Mongoose tells Mr. Ashok: "This is India, not America. There's always a way out here. I told you, we have someone here who works for us—Ramanathan. He's a good fixer" (*The White Tiger* 121).

Globalisation has embraced the developing nations like India, the result of which is that the rich are becoming richer and the poor poorer. Humanitarian approach has lost its way in the jungle of materialism. Mall culture welcomes a rich man, not a poor man. A man with sandals is not allowed in the mall because of his poverty. His crying: "Am I not a human being too?" (*The White Tiger* 148) reveals the heinous face of globalisation which neglects human values. A poor driver is forced to take the responsibility of the master's hit-and-run case. The jail full of drivers reveals a different story. The judges who know the reality keep mum because of their involvement in the racket. Balram tells the truth about the judges: "The judges? Wouldn't they see through this obviously forced confession? But they are in the racket too. They take their bribe, they ignore the discrepancies in the case. And life goes on. For everyone but the driver" (*The White Tiger* 170). The rich men escape from punishment with the help of judges whom they bribe. This is the mockery of the judicial system under the democratic set-up. Here, justice is delayed and the poor do not get justice. Such a situation forces them to take up arms and embrace Naxalism against the rich or the exploiters. In India, traditional values are crushed under the feet of modernity—so-called globalisation. "Everything's coming apart in this country. Families, marriages—everything" (*The White Tiger* 215). The day is not far when there will be a civil war. What will be the future of the country where people start beating the judges in their courtrooms?

Communism is against capitalism which makes the gap wider between the rich and the poor. Politicians or powerful people under the democratic set-up misuse the system and manipulate it for their benefits. The war between the rich and the poor is not new. Balram shares with the Premier that "the history of the world is the history of a ten-thousand-year war of brains between the rich and the poor" (*The White Tiger* 254). The Great Socialist manipulates to win the election. He makes emotional statements only to show that he is the well-wisher of the poor and the exploited who need nothing except the basic amenities. He speaks for them to take the people of the dark into his confidence. Very confidently he declares himself to be the voice of the poor and the disenfranchised:

> 'The election shows that the poor will not be ignored. The Darkness will not be silent. There is no water in our taps, and what do you people in Delhi give us? You give us mobile phones. Can a man drink a phone when he is thirty? Women walk for miles every morning to find a bucket of clean—
>
> 'Do you want to become prime minister of India?'
>
> 'Don't ask me such questions. I have no ambitions for myself. I am simply the voice of the poor and the disenfranchised.'
>
> 'But surely, sir—
>
> 'Let me say one last word, if I may. All I have ever wanted was an India where any boy in any village could dream of becoming the prime minister. Now, as I was saying, women walk for...'

> According to the radio, the ruling party had been hammered at the polls. A new set of parties had come to power. The Great Socialist's party was one of them. He had taken the votes of a big part of the Darkness.
>
> (*The White Tiger* 269)

Balram thinks that nothing could be done to improve the condition of Indian people who wish to be in the rooster coop. The rooster coop—sometimes in the form of traditional Indian family system or sometimes in the form of circumstances—forces them to remain in it. Only one who does not care for the ruin of the family because of the initiative of doing something different can break the rooster coop.

Adiga has highlighted the loopholes of the judicial system. He may be partially right. The Western specs make him see the partial view. The fact is that the judicial system is right but the way it is manipulated is wrong. The enforcement of the legal system has been made it difficult for a layman who avoids it and remains exploited because it is too expensive. The delay in justice mocks at the judicial system which has been stained by the officials who are tempted in favour of the rich or the powerful. Justice is fractured by such manipulators. Actually the fault is not of the system but of the corrupt way it is operated. Adiga rejects outright the parliamentary system. Nowhere does he talk of its reformation or any hope that may remove its drawbacks. What he has got is the right of saying anything in the name of self-examination. Is this the way of improvement? He praises communism and the last portion of the novel clearly favours it. Is communism the only way to remove the loopholes of the democratic system? Is it possible that each voice will be heard and properly represented in communism? Will the unheard voice change the unjust situation? The answer is almost negative. Better to walk on the known path than to walk on the unknown. India is a rich country with rich resources which are supposed to be exploited for the benefit of the poor so that there may be economic growth and the sense of justice may be maintained. But, to hold democracy responsible for the plight of the poor is not a proper excuse.

If Adiga had talked or suggested the way to b:ıng social justice in a democratic set-up, he would have done something substantial. But, to do the postmortem in the name of self-examination and leave the body open is against moral etiquettes. The principle of justice is the foundation on which the democratic building rests. Adiga's protagonist Balram Halwai talks of inequalities between the rich and the poor but how to reduce it is not in his vocabulary. These days, corrupt people or politicians fear because of the people's awakening to their rights. This awakening has been brought about by democracy, which has become a school of learning for the protection of their rights. Democracy is the best alternative left to the people in the present-day scenario for providing rights—be they civil, political, social or economic. In spite of its shortcomings, it is the best government that treats all individuals as equal. Basically, in a democratic set-up, all individuals are "alike or equal" but the best among the equals reign over others. To some extent, it is true that it becomes, to use Maxey's words, a victim of "demagoguism, bossism, and pressure politics" (Political Theory 451) but, even then, it cannot be rejected due to these defects. It is better to bring social justice than to curse the democracy for not having it in spite of its promise. Adiga must keep in mind that India is reputed for being the largest successful democracy in the world. If democracy fails to work in any country, it is not the fault of democracy but of the people responsible for its working. To leave democracy for any other form of government seems to be ridiculous because, to put in C.D. Burns' words, "if an automobile does not work well, it is foolish to go back to a farm cart, however romantic" (*Political Theory* 454). If Adiga's protagonist is taken seriously, one will conclude that India is a faltering nation where one cannot live with self-respect because of democratic system which has become a total failure in providing justice and supporting the spirit of the entrepreneurship. He may not like democracy because of the fractured structure which he sees through the Western microscope but people in India will not leave its spirit. It does not matter if Balram abuses calling it "fucking parliamentary system" responsible for India's backwardness, but, every Indian who is not Balram Halwai in executing his plan that leads to anarchy, seems to say, in Edward Carpenter's words, "O, disrespectable democracy, I love thee". (*Political Theory* 462).

Works Cited

Adiga, Aravind. *The White Tiger*. New Delhi: HarperCollins, 2008. **Print.**

Asirvatham, Eddy. *Political Theory*. New Delhi: S. Chand & Company, 1988. **Print.**

7

The Marxist Roaring

An author, notwithstanding of his objectivity in conception and execution, leaves somewhere the traces of his subjectivity. Some impressions and observations that enter the subconscious level get expressions even unconsciously. One cannot disassociate with the literary creation on the plea that it is objective and does not represent the writer's view anywhere. Post-modernism provides a plea that not one character but various characters articulate their voices and their voices remain authentic to them respectively. But, somewhere, the author favours a particular ideology in spite of his claim to be objective and detached. Aravind Adiga's *The White Tiger* which is said to be a post-modernist novel reveals the traces that the author has a mindset for a particular ideology. *The White Tiger* reveals the Marxist idiom and, in spite of his claim for objectivity, he makes Balram Halwai his mouthpiece for Marxism, an ideology which he thinks better in the present-day world than democracy which is severely criticised. With preconceived notions, he has framed a plan for *The White Tiger* in order to demonstrate the victory of communism and the defeat of democracy. Characters, incidents, backgrounds etc.—all these are presented in the flashlight of Marxism.

Marx (1818-1883), who is the founder of modern communism, has articulated the history of working-class movement in *The Communist Manifesto* (in collaboration with Engels) and the economic theories in *Das Kapital*. He reacted against capitalism and took the world by surprise through his theory 'Marxism' better known as communism. This is the most contested term because of its multiple interpretations.

"Communism, an economic and political system whose goals are total government control of the economy and total income redistribution with the ultimate aim of a classless society, is one of the most misunderstood and feared ideologies. And yet its avowed goal—the establishment of an egalitarian society-has been the ideal of some of the world's best minds and hearts through the centuries" (*Contemporary Society* 425). Communism is said to be the antidote of capitalism. It is against "private ownership of the means of production, private enterprise and private profit", the characteristic features embraced by the capitalism that talks of profit out of production. It is communism which promises to meet "the three great needs of the world: economic security, social or national security, and freedom for self-expression" (Ashirvatham 588) which remain unfulfilled in modern capitalism.

For Marx, matter is more important than spirit. It is matter that determines everything in life. The productive forces make the foundation or the substructure on which the superstructure with religion, moral and politics rests. Surplus value, class struggle, dialectic materialism, classless society and withering away of the state are the popular terms in the Marxist parlance. Aravind Adiga's *The White Tiger* is a Marxist text to a great extent but his Western upbringing gives some twists to his mindset, the result of which he remains oscillating between Marxism and the global economy. His protagonist Balram Halwai foresees "the future of the world" which for him "lies with the yellow man and brown man" (*The White Tiger* 5). He writes letters to the Chinese Premier to share some tips of the entrepreneurship through his life story which he calls "The Autobiography of a Half-Baked Indian". As he is a man of action, he considers himself "tomorrow" and the Americans "yesterday", and is hopeful that the century will be of China and India that will lead the globe.

The ownership of the land and agriculture resulted in feudalism that takes interest in exploiting the labourers. Landownership was the parameter for deciding the place in the olden times. Asirvatham writes: "At the earlier stage feudalism became the prevailing order and man's place in society was determined by the place he occupied in the economic ladder of land ownership and cultivation. Feudalism gradually gave way to capitalism and labour became a commodity to be bought and sold like any other commodity. Instead of destroying slavery, capitalism perpetuates it in a disguised form and the wage-earner becomes a wage-slave" (*The Political Theory* 590). The four landowners, namely: Buffalo, Stork, Wild Boar and Raven in the novel, present the view of feudalistic society prevalent at an early stage. Adiga has not called them by their names but by the name of animals because of the animal appetite that they had. The Stork who is the owner of the river flowing outside the village never forgets to take "a cut of every catch of fish caught by every fisherman in the river, and a toll from every boatman who crossed the river to come to our village" (*The White Tiger* 24). The Wild Boar, the brother of the Stork, owns good agricultural land around Laxmangarh. He gives work to the man who not only bows down to touch his feet but also becomes ready to receive the wage which he thinks proper. No one has the right to speak against the low wages. The Raven who owns the rocky hillside takes a cut from the goatherd for the grazing. If goatherd does not have money, he will sodomise him. The next landowner who is known as the Buffalo is the greediest of all because he never forgets to take one-third from the earnings of the rickshaw-pullers for the use of the road. Mark the excerpt for the description of the lifestyle of the landowners:

> All four of the Animals lived in high-walled mansions just outside Laxmangarh—the landlords' quarters. They had their own temples inside the mansions, and their own wells and ponds, and did not need to come out into the village except to feed. Once upon a time, the children of the four Animals went around town in their own cars; Kusum remembered those days. But after the Buffalo's son had been kidnapped by the Naxals—perhaps you've heard about them, Mr Jiabao, since they're Communists, just like you, and go around shooting rich people on principle—the four Animals had sent their sons and daughters away, to Dhanbad or to Delhi. (*The White Tiger* 25)

It is clear that the landowners keep a distance from the common men who are only the means of exploitation for them. They live in the mansions with their own wells and ponds. They come to the village only for exploitation. They face the challenge from the Naxals, the communists who shoot the landowners or their relatives on principle. It is true that in every stage, whenever the exploiters exploit too much, they face the challenge from the exploited. Is it not shocking that a rich man's body is treated like "a premium cotton pillow, white and soft and blank" (*The White Tiger* 26) while the poor man's "life is written on his body, in a sharp pen" (*The White Tiger* 27)? It is the rickshaw-puller, "a human beast of burden" who bears "a pyramid of middle –class flesh—some fat man with his fat wife and all their shopping bags and groceries" (*The White Tiger* 27). These landlords do not hesitate in exploiting the labourers to the maximum.

All the members of the protagonist's family work for the Stork as bonded labourers for paying the loan taken for the marriage. Balram, the intelligent student who is called the white tiger by the inspector, has to leave the school for "working in a tea shop. Smashing coals. Wiping tables" (*The White Tiger* 38) as a bonded labour for the payment of the loan. When Balram becomes the driver and goes to ask for the job of a driver, the Stork offers him the job because he is young and can be exploited for a long time. The Stork says: "Catch'em young, and you can keep 'em for life. A driver in his forties, you get, what, twenty years of service, then his eyes fail. This fellow will last thirty, thirty-five years. His teeth are solid, he's got his hair, he's in good shape" (*The White Tiger* 66). This is the way the landowner thinks about the poor. They are always one step ahead of the poor for whom they make plans. Mr Ashok promises to give Balram the money for the wedding expenditure. Balram thinks and concludes that these rich people will not hesitate in fucking the wife in the name of generosity. No doubt, he has left the village and come to Delhi but the rich people still own the poor people's "body, soul, and arse" (*The White Tiger* 170).

According to Marx, the three stages through which society passes are (1) primitive communism (2) historical society (present industrial), and (3) higher communism. The third stage combines the communism of the primitive epoch with the technical science and achievements of the historical science and achievements of the historical epoch (Asirvatham 588). The novel *The White Tiger* offers all these three stages prevalent in the society from time to time. India in ancient times was an instance of primitive communism. All lived happily and satisfactorily. The social system was based on the four *pursharthas—dharma*, *artha*, *kama* and *moksha,* and the four *varnas—brahmin*, *kshatriya*, *vaishya* and *shudra*. People worked according to their varnas. Mark the excerpt for the happy and prosperous ancient India:

> See, this country, in its days of greatness, when it was the richest nation on earth, was like a zoo. A clean, well-kept, orderly zoo. Everyone in his place, everyone happy. Goldsmiths here Cowherds here. Landlords there. The man called a Halwai made sweets.The man called a cowherd tended cows. The untouchable cleaned faeces. Landlords were kind to their serfs. Women covered their heads with a veil and turned their eyes to the ground when talking to strange men. (*The White Tiger* 63)

But, when India got freedom, the picture changed. The ancient India gave place to the industrial India. This phase became responsible for creating a wide gap between the rich and the poor. Mark the excerpt for the present industrial stage:

> And then, thanks to all those politicians in Delhi, on the fifteenth of August, 1947—the day the British left—the cages had been let open; and the animals had attacked and ripped each other apart and jungle law replaced zoo law. Those that were the most ferocious, the hungriest, had eaten everyone else up, and grown big bellies. That was all that counted now, the size of your belly. It didn't matter whether you were a woman, or a Muslim, or an untouchable: anyone with a belly could rise up.
>
> (*The White Tiger* 64)

The zoo law of the ancient India gave place to the jungle law that favoured the mighty with a large belly. Hence, "in the old days there were one thousand castes and destinies in India. These days, there are just two castes: 'Men with Big Bellies, and Men with Small Bellies' (*The White Tiger* 64) and two destinies "eat or get eaten up " (*The White Tiger* 64). Now the world comes to the third stage that combines communism of the primitive stage with the present technological advancement. Technology will rule the world. That is why Balram comes to the field of technology in Bangalore and becomes the white tiger. His motto "We Drive Technology Forward" (*The White Tiger* 301) clearly indicates the advancement in technology. How confidently he states:

> If you were sitting here with me, under this big chandelier, I would show you all the secrets of my business. You could stare at the screen of my silver Macintosh laptop and see photos of my SUVs, my drivers, my garages, my mechanics, and my paid-off policemen.
>
> All of them belong to me—Munna, whose destiny was to be a sweet-maker! (*The White Tiger* 302)

He ends his story, telling the Chinese Premier that he will sell everything in the end and will start a school where students will be guided on the lines of communism. Hence, the novel *The White Tiger* reveals the presence of the three Marxian stages, namely, primitive communism and industrial society followed by higher communism.

Religion and institutions like marriage are not in the vocabulary of Marxism. It is man who has created God. For Marx, "Man makes religion; religion does not make man". Religion, he said, is "the opiate of the people"; and God exists only in man's mind (Ashirvatham 587). Family and private property are associated with each other and, hence, are bound to disappear in time. Mutual affection is the only ground on which marriage can rest. Marx does not talk of absolute morality. If there is any morality, it is relative based on the economic perspectives. Aravind Adiga's novel *The White Tiger* mocks at religion; talks of relative morality and also shatters the marriage institution. He mocks at all the religions particularly Hindu religion calling the 36,000,000 crores gods 'arses' and creating a hierarchy among gods worshipped by the people living in the Light and the Darkness. The protagonist shares this with the Chinese Premier, a communist who is not expected to have faith in gods the way Hindus have. Some people do not believe in gods. He is surprised how these gods find their places in the hearts of the people. Gods are politicians who get elected and re-elected year after year. He does not intend to hurt the religious feelings of the Hindus though he actually hurts.

Balram considers Hanuman as the deity of the people living in the darkness. He is the supreme instance of devotion and service to his master Rama. He thinks that religion becomes a rooster coop from which it becomes difficult to come out. People in India are so lost in religion that it is really hard "for a man to win his freedom in India" (*The White Tiger* 19). In one of his soliloquies, he seems to be talking with God in the form of the devil who does not accept His sovereignty. He spits at God again and again to show his hatred for Him. He thinks himself as neither a man nor a demon. He is a woken-up man among the sleepers.

After the murder, Balram goes to Bangalore where he settles with Dharam and does not think of the family. Dharam belongs to the new generation which "is growing up with no moral at all" (*The White Tiger* 316). Balram decides that if Dharam talks of the family, he will kill him. This decision clearly reveals the fact that for Balram who is a true Marxist, family has no meaning. Earlier, when he goes to the village as a driver of Mr Ashok, he is given the best food. But, food does not seem to be food but the flesh from Kishan's body. "There were red, curried bone and flesh in front of me—and it seemed to me that they had served me flesh from Kishan's own body on that plate" (*The White Tiger* 85). It is family that exploits the earning family member. He considers family a rooster coop, out of which he tries to come. Pinky Madam leaves Mr Ashok and later divorces him. Balram Halwai is interested in the harmonious relationship between Pinky Madam and Mr Ashok not because they are husband and wife but because of his future that depends on the couple. "Marriage", no doubt, is "a good institution" but "Everything's coming apart in this country. Families, marriages—everything" (*The White Tiger* 215).

Whatever happens in the world is an outcome of matter. Relationship or status is based on matter. Marx advocates for the change in the various interpretations of the world. For him, "It is not the consciousness of men that determines their existence, but, on the contrary their social existence determines their consciousness" (*Political Thought* 201). Further, he believes that "all the social, political and intellectual relations, all religious and legal systems, all the theoretical outlooks which emerge in the course of history, are derived from the material conditions of life" (*Political Thought* 204). *The White Tiger* exposes the fact that it is not the state that governs but the powerful authorities dominate the state and make it work for their gains, not for the welfare of the poor. A man in sandals is not allowed to enter the mall meant only for the rich. He cries: "Am I not a human being too" (*The White Tiger* 148)? The rich enjoy all the privileges because of matter. It is matter that decides man, not the man matter. Even, Balram Halwai, the driver of Mr Ashok, fears to enter the mall. He gathers courage, changes his dress and enters it through the rear door. But, he is conscious of his poverty and this always reminds him again and again, creating a kind of fear that he will be recognised and then taken out of the mall by the guard. Mark the excerpt that reveals a kind of fugitive life when he enters the mall. "Even as I was walking inside the mall, I was sure someone would say, *Hey! That man is a paid driver*! What's he doing in here? There were guards in grey uniforms on every floor—all of them seemed to be watching me. It was my first taste of the fugitive's life" (*The White Tiger* 152). He succeeds in entering as he is different and not destined to be a slave forever. He is a man who can see the beauty in the world. His father, being a rickshaw-puller, is no better than "a human beast of burden" (*The White Tiger* 27) and that is why he never wishes such a life for his son for whom he has a plan—the plan that he should be a man, not a slave.

Balram goes to the school and makes himself different from others on account of his intelligence. The school inspector calls him the white tiger in the village because he is rare among the village students. The system works according to the capitalist class. Justice is not a divine concept as it is thought of. It is influenced by the dominant class that moves the legal system in its favour. "Legal systems are not the pure manifestations of human or divine reason, but ultimately reflect the interests of the dominant class in particular historical periods" (*Contemporary Literary Theory* 25).

Balram Halwai takes the responsibility of the crime which he has not committed. He signs the bond that he is himself responsible for the hit-and-run case. He is forced to do it for the sake of saving the honour of the Stork family. Balram's family does not make a protest. Going to Tihar Jail for his employer is a sacrifice which every driver is expected to prove himself "loyal as a dog" and be branded as "the perfect servant" (*The White Tiger* 170). The judges know the truth but they keep mum because they are bought by the dominating class.

Life continues to flow for everyone but not for the driver who has to live not for himself but for the employer. Mark the excerpt for the pain that Balram expresses: "The judges? Wouldn't they see through this obviously forced confession? But they are in the racket too. They take their bribe, they ignore the discrepancies in the case. And life goes on. For everyone but the driver" (*The White Tiger* 170). He feels himself as an ass but does not wish that his children should be asses like him and carry "rubble around for the rich" (*The White Tiger* 193). It is the rooster coop that works from inside making him realise his social status of being a servant. The poor get with obligation what is left by the rich.

Balram spends money for having a foreign girl with golden hair but, in return, he is deceived as he gets a girl with painted hair. Then, he realises that it is the dominant class that gets the best:

> He pushed the door open. A chandelier, a widow, a green bed—and a girl with golden hair sitting on the bed.
>
> I sighed, because this one looked nothing like Kim Basinger. Not half as pretty. That was when it hit me—

> in a way it never had before—how the rich always get the best things in life, and all that we get is their leftovers.
>
> (*The White Tiger* 233)

The dominating class gets the upper hand and rules over the poor. Matter determines the social consciousness, not the social consciousness matter. Later, Balram steals Mr Ashok's red bag full of money and becomes the dominating figure. Matter gives him a dominant position and a power to sway the people.

Circumstances do not make man; man makes circumstances. No principle decides whether the action is good or bad. It is circumstance that determines the action. Good action, for Marx, is "action appropriate to the circumstances" and "circumstances change and new circumstances of course demand new study" (*Political Thought* 199). The difference between a rich and poor man is that a rich man recognises what is beautiful while a poor man does not. Balram Halwai loves to recall the lines of Iqbal, the great poet. "The moment you recognise what is beautiful in this world, you stop being a slave" (*The White Tiger* 276). If every poor boy is taught how to paint, he will think of beautiful which will make "the end of the rich in India" (*The White Tiger* 276). The problem with the poor in India is that they find circumstances as rooster coop and do not think to come out of them. But, it is not so with the protagonist who does not wish to remain a servant forever. He changes circumstances that help him to rise from the slavery to the status of a free man. He feels "rage" (*The White Tiger* 230), not guilty in cheating his employer. He feels that he is taking only what Mr Ashok has snatched from him, i.e. a man like him. He is so determined now with a decision that when the other driver asks him about his master, he tells him that he is his own master. Such a response from Balram makes the driver hug him with the title "man". It is ambition that makes him create circumstances in his favour, and certainly his determination helps him to rise from the status of a driver to the status of an entrepreneur. It does not mean that the poor do not dream; they dream but do not create circumstances in order to translate the dream into reality. The rich who make circumstances in their favour also dream of "losing weight and looking like the poor" (*The White Tiger* 225) but do not get it translated into reality. Thus, the dreams of the rich and the dreams of the poor do not overlap, and their dreams remain dreams as ever. The poor men dream of being rich without creating circumstances while the rich men create circumstances for growing richer but do not labour like labourers to look like them in physique, and so their dream of looking like the poor in physique remains a dream.

India is a rich country with poor people. Concentration of wealth in a few hands is responsible for poverty. The rich are becoming richer and the poor poorer. Technology has decreased the demand of the labour, the result of which is "a pool of unemployed which keeps down wages, and the lot of the workers becomes harder and harder to bear until "they have nothing to lose but their chains" (*Political Thought* 211). The two classes—the property owners and wage-earners—are against each other. The further increase in poverty will lead to the class struggle, which for Marx, will result in "the triumph of the oppressed" (*Political Thought* 212). *The White Tiger* demonstrates the unemployed labourers who seem to be hopeless. Mark the excerpt for the unemployment:

> Things are different in the Darkness. There, every morning, tens of thousands of young men sit in the tea shops, reading the newspaper, or lie on a charpoy humming a tune, or sit in their rooms talking to a photo of a film actress. They have no job to do today. They know they won't get any job today. They've given up the fight.
>
> (*The White Tiger* 54)

Labourers are not labourers but "the human spiders" (*The White Tiger* 88). Balram sees men working at tea shops on the river bank and find that in spite of being mature, they always remain boys throughout their life. Corrupt politicians are also responsible for such a miserable state of the poor people. Balram knows about the Great Socialist who takes bribery for any work and transfers "that money into a bank account in a small, beautiful country in Europe full of white people and black money" (*The White Tiger* 98). If this black money is brought back to India, it will solve the problem of poverty to a great extent. No doubt, India is progressing but the poor people remain as they are. Then, who is taking the advantage of this progress? Certainly, the rich people. But, Balram believes in the principles of Marx. He takes the red bag full of money and uses it to grow rich. He is interested in producing the white tiger like him. Certainly the poor will raise their voice leading to class struggle which will lead them to their victory.

Surplus value, a popular term in Marxist terminology is the difference between the values of wages—which a labourer produces and which he actually gets. If a capitalist appropriates surplus value, it is a theft. It is "concealed labour" or "labour not paid for" (Asirvatham 591). In India, the rich people are guilty of appropriating the surplus value of the poor labourer. A driver is not a driver in India though he is paid for being a driver. He is driver-cum-servant who performs all kinds of menial jobs but is paid only for being a driver. Not to pay a person for all the pieces of work is a theft on the part of the rich. Balram shares this with the Chinese Premier: "Now, I say they took me on as their 'driver'. I don't exactly know how you organise your servants in China. But in India—or, at least, in the Darkness- the rich don't have drivers, cooks, barbers, and tailors. They simply have servants" (*The White Tiger* 68-69). Mr Ashok makes Pinky understand the value of Indian servants saying that no one expects in New York that the servant will bring tea and biscuits while the master is still sleeping. It happens in India that a servant becomes a family servant. He is blackmailed in the name of family member. It is Ram Bahadur, a guard who not only performs the duty of being a guard but also performs other menial work of the family. The labour that he does in performing other roles remains unpaid. Mr Ashok discusses with Pinky Madam and says: "Where in New York will you find someone to bring you tea and sweet biscuits while you're still lying in bed, the way Ram Bahadur does for us? You know, he's been in my family for thirty years—we call him a servant, but he's part of the family" (*The White Tiger* 89). He bribes the politicians to evade the income tax. The tax which is meant for the development so that the poor may also take an advantage is either paid partially or remains unpaid. Pinky Madam hands over a brown envelope as a tip to Balram for taking her to the airport. When he opens it, he finds forty-seven hundred rupees. He muses over this odd figure. His reflection shows the mentality of the rich who give less money than they initially think to offer. Mark the excerpt for a different kind of surplus value which is pocketed by Pinky Madam who initially thought of putting more money in the envelope than she actually put for Balram Halwai:

> Forty-seven hundred rupees. In that brown envelope under my bed.
>
> Odd sum of money—wasn't it? There was a mystery to be solved here. Let's see. Maybe she started off giving me five thousand, and then, being cheap, like all rich people are—remember how the Mongoose made me get down on my knees for that one-rupee coin?—deducted three hundred.
>
> *That's not how the rich think, you moron. Haven't you learned yet?*
>
> She must have taken out ten thousand at first. Then cut it in half, and kept half for herself. Then taken out another hundred, and another hundred. That's how cheap they are.
>
> *So that means they really owe you ten thousand. But if she thought she owed you ten thousand, then what she truly owned you was, what—ten times more?*
>
> (*The White Tiger* 206)

Rich people are cheap and poor with heavy riches in their pockets. Their pockets grow fatter and fatter because of the theft that they commit in not paying the labour what it deserves. Balram again cites one more example that exposes the mentality of the rich people who give less than they initially think to offer.

> 'Balram. You'll need some money, won't you?'
>
> 'Sir, no. There's no need of that.'
>
> 'Wait, Balram. Let me take out my wallet. You're a good member of the family. You never ask for more money—I know that other drivers are constantly asking for overtime

> and insurance: but you never say a word. You're old-fashioned. I like that. We'll take care of all the wedding expenses, Balram. Here, Balram—here's ... here's...'
>
> I saw him take out a thousand-rupee note, put it back, then take out a five-hundred, then put it back, and take out a hundred.
>
> Which he handed to me. (*The White Tiger* 258)

Mr Ashok takes Balram into confidence and wishes to give him money for his wedding expenses. Initially he takes out a one thousand rupee note but in the end offers him only one hundred rupee. These rich people have nothing to give to the poor people but they have sufficient money to offer in bribery. Balram sees his master Mr Ashok going from one bank to the other bank to withdraw money for bribery. The money is in the red bag which becomes heavier from one bank to the other bank. Mark the excerpt for depiction of the red bag that contained seven hundred thousand rupees:

> We went from bank to bank, and the weight of the red bag grew. I felt its pressure increase on my lower back—as if I were taking Mr Ashok and his bag not in a car, but the way my father would take a customer and his bag—in a rickshaw.
>
> Seven hundred thousand rupees.
>
> It was enough for a house. A motorbike. And a small shop.
>
> A new life.
>
> *My* seven hundred thousand rupees.
>
> (*The White Tiger* 280-281)

The red bag containing the money belongs to him not to Mr Ashok who was going to offer the money to the politicians to evade from the income tax mess. It is the money of the unpaid labour that the rich people like Mr Ashok put in their pocket. Hence, Balram calls the red bag containing money his own. *"See—Mr Ashok is giving money to all these politicians in Delhi so that they will excuse him from the tax he has to pay. And who owns that tax, in the end? Who but the ordinary people of this country—you"* (*The White Tiger* 244)!

Class struggle and revolution are the two essential driving forces that change the way of history. Revolution becomes a necessity on all levels—be it social or political or legal or technological or historical. Class war has always been crucial to the history of society. The protagonist Balram shares this fact with the Chinese Premier: "Mr Premier, I won't be saying anything new if I say that the history of the world is the history of a ten-thousand-year war of brains between the rich and the poor" (*The White Tiger* 254). It is capitalism that offers thesis; organised labour reacts to it and becomes anti-thesis and finally both thesis and anti-thesis result in synthesis in the form of classless society.

Marx pictures human life as "a grim struggle between the capitalists and wage-earners; that is between the bourgeoisie and the proletariat" (*Political Theory* 592). Working classes come tighter against the common exploiters. The closing words of the *Communist Manifesto* which carry with them an oratorical flourish are: "The Communists disdain to conceal their views and aims. They openly declare that their ends can be attained only by the forcible overthrow of all existing social conditions. Let the ruling classes tremble at the prospect of a communist revolution. The proletarians have nothing to lose but their chains. They have a world to win. Working men of all countries, unite" (*Political Theory* 593). The revolution that eliminates the bourgeoisie results in the dictatorship of the proletariat that will destroy state and capital system leading to a classless society.

In *The White Tiger*, the Naxals, the communists in ideology, have raised the weapons against the rich people like the Four Animals. The poor in India do not think of class war because "99.9 per cent of us are caught in the Rooster Coop just like those poor guys in the poultry market" (*The White Tiger* 175). A servant does not steal the suitcase full of diamond though "he's no Gandhi, he's human" like all but he is in "the Rooster coop" that works so forcefully on him that he never thinks of theft. "The trustworthiness of servants is the basis of the entire Indian economy" (*The White Tiger* 175). Does it not seem to be shocking that "a handful of men in the country have trained the remaining 99.9 percent—as strong, as talent, as intelligent in every way—to exist in perpetual servitude; a servitude so strong that you can put the key of his emancipation in man's hands and he will throw it back at you with a curse" (*The White Tiger* 176). Generally the poor are satisfied with their condition and do not think of revolt against the exploitation. When it crosses the limit of their tolerance and no option is left for them, they think of taking weapons like the Naxals do. A man of pervert nature can think of revolt against the dominating class. A man who cares for the family can never think of taking such a drastic step of revolt. Balram himself admits: "only a man who is prepared to see his family destroyed—hunted, beaten, and burned alive by the masters—can break out of the coop. That would take no normal human being, but a freak, a pervert of nature" (*The White Tiger* 176-77).

Marxism talks of revolution, and *The Communist Manifesto* emphasises not on the reformation but on the revolution for the proletariat. "It is a call for the working class to adopt certain tactics, highly flexible in kind and changing with changing in circumstances, but consistent in their revolutionary purpose" (*Political Thought* 198). This is the only revolution that provides the dominance of the working class, ultimately resulting in classless society and the destruction of the state. Balram Halwai states: "Maybe once in a hundred years there is a revolution that frees the poor" (*The White Tiger* 303). He proudly feels that he is also "a part of all that is changing in this country" (*The White Tiger* 318). He has succeeded "in the struggle that every poor man here should be making—the struggle not to take the lashes your father took, not to end up in a mound of indistinguishable bodies that will rot in the black mud of Mother Ganga" (*The White Tiger* 318). He has to murder his master to establish himself as a man—a white tiger. "All I wanted was the change to be a man—and for that, one murder was enough" (*The White Tiger* 318). After three or four years, he will sell everything and start a school for poor children in order to make them white tigers who will not be allowed "to corrupt anyone's head with prayers and stories about God or Gandhi—nothing but the facts of life" (*The White Tiger* 319). He dreams of a classless society that will have the people with facts so that they may differentiate between men and animals. "Let animals live like animals; let humans live like humans" (*The White Tiger* 276) is the sole philosophy that he wishes to translate in the classless and stateless society. He is sure of the victory of communism over capitalism when he forecasts that the white men will be finished in twenty years, yielding place to the yellow men and brown men to rule the whole world.

No one can deny the fact that Balram actually articulates Aravind Adiga's Marxist ideology. He follows Marx's doctrine that will bring progress and triumph of man as man. He seems to claim what Engels claimed: "Man has only to know himself, to measure all conditions of life against himself, to judge them by his own character, to organise the world according to the demands of his own nature in a truly human way, and he will have solved all the riddles of our age," is Engel's proud claim" (*Political Thought* 205). His protagonist Balram is a role model for his workers who are treated as workers only, not members of family. But, it is surprising that Adiga makes Balram "ready to have children" (*The White Tiger* 321) in spite of considering marriage a rooster coop. Why Balram, who is interested in dipping his, 'beak' into beautiful girls becomes ready to be in the rooster coop is not in tune with Marxism. Relationship, feelings, love, sentiments etc. are not in his dictionary. Actually this is not the fault of Balram but of his creator who embraces Marxism with his body leaving his soul for capitalism for the immense pleasure. The red colour is mixed with white, the result of which is that it has become pink—neither pure red nor pure white. He knows that he cannot neglect the pink colour that paints only human passions, sentiments and emotions notwithstanding Marx's exaggerating claim for the economic factor. Truly, he has married Marxism legally but continued to have illicit relations with capitalism. That's why Adiga's *The White Tiger* is a Marxist text despite some deviations.

Works Cited

Adiga, Aravind. *The White Tiger*. New Delhi: HarperCollins, 2008. **Print**.

Asirvatham, Eddy. *Political Theory*. New Delhi: S. Chand and Company, 1988. **Print**.

Perry, John A. & Erna K. Perry. *Contemporary Society*. New York: HaperCollins, 1991. **Print**.

Selden, Raman. *A Reader's Guide to Contemporary Literary Theory*. Lexington, Kentucky: The University Press of Kentucky, 1989. **Print.**

Wayper, C. L. *Political Thought*. London: The English Universities Press Ltd. 1954, rpt. 1958. **Print.**

8

The Great Indian Rooster Coop

> The Great Indian Rooster Coop. Do you have something like it in China too? I doubt it, Mr Jiabao. (175)

A human being, being a part of society, does not deviate from the setrules and norms of the society. One who deviates and floats against the flow becomes sometimes trendsetter and also sometimes a creator of problems. It is a fact that progress occurs because of the new inventions and new discoveries which occur only when one thinks and acts differently from others. People do not favour such persons for their initiative in thought and action. Any new thought, if it leads to a better outcome for society, is a welcome sign for progress but if it leads to the path of destruction and hurts humanity it should certainly be criticised.

Generally people do not like change and wish to remain as they are. The way of living and behaving sets the culture of the people who followed some certain norms, rules and parameters. It is Indian culture that the quality of synthesis is based on the principle of cosmopolitanism. It talks of the soul without neglecting the body. People of all religions live here peacefully and harmoniously. Relationship is not based on material gains but on emotional bond. Marriage here is not a contract of two bodies but a union of two souls. People follow their respective religions. No religion insults and humiliates the people of other religions. It is the culture—Indian culture—that is in the blood of every Indian. Destructive elements that follow no religion remain present in every country for destabilising the stability, and disturbing the peace and communal harmony. These are the positive points of Indian culture that make a man and restrain him from being an animal. But, some certain people revolt against any set parameter—be it religious or social or political or any other. In the name of freedom, they do not wish to be fettered like others. Aravind Adiga is one of those people who think that these set-parameters of Indian society are no better than the rooster coop. His protagonist Balram Halwai shares with the Chinese Premier and holds the Great Indian Rooster Coop responsible for the miserable condition of the Indian people who are satisfied with life and remain inside it. Because of the coop, they can never be free people in spite of getting freedom from the British rule. Adiga has used the rooster coop as a metaphor that reflects the Indians' mindset. Though he holds the coop responsible for mental slavery, it seems that he himself is in the Marxian coop which confines his mind that thinks and acts accordingly.

The Rooster Coop is the metaphor that runs throughout the text of *The White Tiger* which demonstrates the way it works in India to tame the Indians. Balram Halwai, the protagonist, is a white tiger that cannot be confined in the coop, and with the passage of time, breaks the coop and becomes the master. He reflects over India's past and finds that "The greatest thing to come out of this country in the ten thousand years of its history is the Rooster Coop" (173). He clarifies this term to the Chinese Premier in the letter and states:

> Go to Old Delhi, behind the Jama Masjid, and look at the way they keep chickens there in the market. Hundreds of pale hens and brightly coloured roosters, stuffed tightly into wire-mesh cages, packed as tightly as worms in a belly, pecking each other and shitting on each other, jostling just for breathing space; the whole cage giving off a horrible stench—the stench of terrified, feathered flesh. On the wooden desk above this coop sits a grinning young butcher, showing off the flesh and organs of a recently chopped-up chicken, still oleaginous with a coating of dark blood. The roosters in the coop smell the blood from above. They see the organs of their brothers lying around them. They know they're next. Yet they do not rebel. They do not try to get out of the coop.

> The very same thing is done with human beings in this country. (173-74)

The description is scatological in nature, and the similarity between chickens and human beings is too much. Does it really happen so? Do people see other people being butchered without reacting to inhuman activity? Do people really not rebel and try to come out of the coop? Every person has a limit for tolerance and crossing the line makes him a rebel. Will Adiga, the butcher, continue to chop the Indian culture on the Western slab? Does he think that the people of India will not react to this derogatory act?

Balram finds the Indians to be "the world's most honest people" and thinks that it is so because 99.9 per cent of them are "caught in the Rooster Coop like those poor guys in the poultry market" (175). The remaining 0.1 per cent have become the masters because either they broke the coop or never entered it. These free people guide the people in the coop on how to remain a servant forever. They have inserted slavery in their mind so much that they will throw the key of freedom if one gives. Surprisingly he states:

> Never before in human history have so few owed so much to so many, Mr Jiabao. A handful of men in the country have trained the remaining 99.9 percent—as strong, as talent, as intelligent in every way—to exist in perpetual servitude; a servitude so strong that you can put the key of his emancipation in man's hands and he will throw it back at you with a curse. (175- 76)

Adiga has treated the metaphor of rooster coop in various ways. A family, because of its emotional charms, also works as rooster coop. Balram is given the money for learning driving on condition that he will look after the family when he earns. He is expected to send money when he gets the job of a chauffeur in the Stork family. He is chastised for not sending money to the family. The granny Kusum blackmails him emotionally. "My grandson has a job, and he still forces me to work. This is the fate of an old woman in this world" (84). As he is out of her control, she thinks of his marriage for taming him. She declares that she has found a girl for him and informs him that "the moment she has her menstrual cycle, she can come here" (85). After the death of his father, Kishan is the only earning member in the family. When Balram gets the chance to come to the village, he feels disgusted to see the condition of his brother Kishan who was being eaten by the family. He is served food which seems to him flesh from Kishan's body. "There were red, curried bone and flesh in front of me—and it seemed to me that they had served me flesh from Kishan's own body on that plate" (85). This is the bad effect in the joint family that the earning member is exploited to the maximum. As he is a tiger that remains free, he does not like this family system and later in the novel he forgets the family in order to be rich and prosperous. He declares in the letter to the Chinese Premier that "*the Indian family*, is the reason we are trapped and tied to the coop" (176). Marriage is the link that makes family. Kusum tempts Balram Halwai for marriage so that he may be tamed for further exploitation. A man fails to think differently if he marries because family becomes the priority. Great ideas or great things come from unmarried people who can think openly, unhesitatingly and differently. Marriage becomes the corollary in making the family as the great Indian rooster coop that cages the man and never lets him go out. The Western touch intends to weaken the institution of marriage and frees him for independent thinking. It is Pinky Madam who leaves Mr Ashok and later divorces him. When the Fat man comes to know Mr Ashok's divorce in process, he sympathises with him saying that "marriage is a good institution" but "everything's coming apart in this country. Families, marriages—everything" (215).

In ancient India, the *varna vyavastha* with *Brahmin*, *vaishya*, *kshatriya* and *shudra* was prevalent. Everyone knew his or her role according to this system. For Adiga, this system was just like a zoo that had cages with animals inside them. Everyone was caged in the *varna vyavastha*. Mark the excerpt for the *varna vyavastha* which was no better than a coop:

> See, this country, in its days of greatness, when it was the richest nation on earth, was like a zoo. A clean, well-kept,

> orderly zoo. Everyone in his place, everyone happy. Goldsmiths here Cowherds here. Landlords there. The man called a Halwai made sweets. The man called a cowherd tended cows. The untouchable cleaned faeces. Landlords were kind to their serfs. Women covered their heads with a veil and turned their eyes to the ground when talking to strange men. (63)

A person who is known as halwai is supposed to be a sweet-maker. When Balram Halwai goes to meet the old driver for learning driving, he interrogates him regarding the caste and exclaims how a Halwai can learn driving. He shares with the Chinese Premier and tells him the name 'Halwai' means sweet maker. The caste becomes destiny. It is the caste that types a man in spite of his longing for a different job. He states:

> See: Halwai, my name, means 'sweet-maker'.
>
> That's my caste—my destiny. Everyone in the Darkness who hears that name knows all about me at once. That's why Kishan and I kept getting jobs at sweetshops wherever we went. The owner thought, *Ah, they're Halwais, making sweets and tea is in their blood.* (63)

Caste also confines a man and, hence, becomes a coop. A Halwai, as the caste indicates, is fit only for making sweets or things like tea that are expected from him. Because of this mentality a man neither thinks nor imagines anything that is outside the coop.

The rooster coop is strengthened by the religious feelings that make a man crippled to the extent that he remains passive and treads the trodden path without producing anything original or new. Hindu religion confines the people in the coop by offering the ideals of Rama, Sita and Hanuman. Hanuman becomes the best instance of devotion and servant. People from the darkness worship Hanuman and take him to be their ideal. Hence, they remain servants like Hanuman and never think of replacing their masters. He says to the Chinese Premier: "These are the kinds of gods they have foisted on us, Mr Jiabao. Understand, now, how hard it is for a man to win his freedom in India" (19). While serving the Stork family, he considers Mr

Ashok as Rama, Pinky Madam as Sita and himself as Hanuman. He says: "I would drive them wherever they wanted, as faithfully as the servant-god Hanuman carried about his master and mistress, Ram and Sita" (46). Ideals are offered to the people so that they may feel satisfied while remaining in the coop. But, this Hanuman like Balram, later in the novel, does the work of Ravana. He is not born to be a servant and so thinks of breaking the rooster coop. He associates himself with a man in the khaki uniform who spits at God. His throwing of the stickers of deities on the body of Mr Ashok is the throwing of religion. This rejection opens the gate of the coop and makes him free. As he is different from the common people, he comes out of the religious coop successfully and gets settled in Bangalore as an entrepreneur.

Capital possesses the power of controlling labour. It is capital that forces man to be a slave. Sometimes a man does not wish to be in the coop but he becomes a victim of circumstances that compel him to be in. Hence, circumstances also become the rooster coop that makes man slave. The protagonist Balram has to work as a bonded labour not because he has done something but simply because his family took a loan for the wedding and failed to repay. All the members of the family work for the Stork family in return of the loan. He has to leave the school for "Working in a tea shop. Smashing coals. Wiping tables" (38).

When he becomes a driver, he does not ask for money because for him his masters and mistress are "like a father and mother" and he cannot ask for money from his parents. A driver does not perform the job of a driver only, he is expected to do all kinds of work. He does it without raising his voice. No doubt, India is free but the people are still slaves in spite of getting freedom. Why do they wish to remain servants? Why do they not think of taking the place of their masters? It is slavery that is deep-rooted in them. Hence, he says: "I don't understand why other people don't buy chandeliers all the time, and put them up everywhere. Free people don't know the value of freedom, that's the problem" (117). The protagonist is happy and satisfied with what his master gives. He tells the man with diseased lips that he (Balram) gets enough money from his master. He proves himself that he is "a loyal servant to the end" (123). He wears the uniform of a driver and looks like a monkey while the drivers in cities or town do not like to wear uniforms. He wears it because he wishes to be looked at so. When Pinky Madam leaves him behind, he does not show his anger but rather makes her believe that he is not angry and can never be so because "employers are like mother and father" (162). It is the desire to be a servant that has penetrated deeply into him. Religion, family, ideals etc. are mentioned in order to make the servant ideal to the extent that he never thinks of coming out of the coop. These are the ideals which make the master confident of his servant with a "suitcase full of diamonds" in spite of the fact that "He's no Gandhi, he's human" (175). What makes him honest to the core is the Rooster Coop that trains the servants to be trustworthy. China may have secret police or dictatorship but in India they are not needed because of the Rooster Coop. The Rooster Coop works with a lot of money but when there is question of a few rupees, it fails. It fails because it tempts to be corrupted. But, so far as there is a question of big money, they are honest. Here, in India, "Masters trust servants with diamonds" (175).

It is the well planning of the rich to create the coop for the poor so that they may remain inside it forever and never think of their release from it. Even a magazine like *Murder Weekly* is made available to every poor at the rate of four and a half rupees. The stories of murder, rape and revenge make the servants think of "strangling their bosses" (125). But, the reading of the magazine is safe as it does not give birth to any danger because the end of the stories prove to be a coop which makes them think of the consequence. The more they think the more they become paralysed in their determination. The real danger begins when the driver "starts to read Gandhi and the Buddha" because their thoughts make them think about slavery and the possible ways to come out of the coop. It is not only the magazine that deactivates their rebellious thought but even a weight machine also plays its part in strengthening the power of the coop. Balram weighs himself on the machine which releases a chit on which the weight 59 and a note "Respect for the law is the first command of the gods" are written. He laughs at the tricks of the rich who have misused even the machine for creating the coop. What he has done is just the opposite of what is written on the fortune-telling chit. He states: "I let the fortune-telling chit fall on the floor and I laughed. Even here, in the weight machine of a train station, they try to hoodwink us. Here, on the threshold of man's freedom, just before he boards a train to a new life, their flashing fortune machines are the final alarm bell of the Rooster Coop" (248). In India, moral consciousness has been etched so deep in the psyche that a man feels guilty when he murders a man. "murder a man, and you feel responsible for his life—possessive, even" (46).

It is the capital that makes all the differences. It makes a poor culture and creates an inferiority complex among the poor. Balram living in the village is not taught to lead a decent and cultured life. Pinky Madam makes fun of him and tells him that he is not a man but an uncivilised monkey. He scratches his groin and never brushes his teeth because his father never taught these things. He states: "Why had my father never told me not to scratch my groin? Why had my father never taught me to brush my teeth in milky foam? Why had he raised me to live like an animal? Why do all the poor live amid such filth, such ugliness?" (151). He finds himself in the cage of inferiority complex created by rich people like Pinky Madam and Mr Ashok. He regrets his past and feels that if "a man could spit his past out so easily" (151). It is the capital responsible for creating economic inequalities. A man with capital is a human being, otherwise his life is no better than an animal. A poor man in sandals is not allowed to enter a mall because he is not treated as a human being. Balram is a different man and knows the way to tackle such a situation. He makes up his mind to enter the mall but as a driver he cannot enter and so takes a new, white T-shirt, wears it and enters the mall through the rear entrance. But, as long as he is there, he tastes "the fugitive life" (152) because of fear of the guards in gray uniform. Poverty itself becomes a rooster coop that makes man lead the life of a slave. Even the democratic system works in strengthening the coop. How many poor people do use their voting rights in spite of their claim of adult franchise? Politicians lure the poor people in the name of bringing light through electricity, water-taps and education in the area of darkness. The Great Socialist claims to be "the voice of the poor and the disenfranchised" (269) while the reality is that no one cares for the development of the village. The poor are left to their own miserable condition. People do not vote but their voting rights are used by others. Balram never goes to the booth but his vote is used by others.

The democratic system also gives liberty to the judicial system in giving the decision in favour of the rich. Balram is to go to jail for the crime that has been committed by Pinky Madam. It seems that the rich masters have an absolute right over the body of their servants. "We have left the villages, but the masters still own us, body, soul, and arse" (170). He does not even think of running away or telling the truth to the judge that he is not guilty. Such ideas do not enter his mind because of the rooster coop which is "guarded from the inside".

Balram Halwai does not get energy and enthusiasm to come out of the coop at random but his own father's guidance and circumstances force him to break it. When his father comes to know that Balram has come from school, he feels angry and shouts at Kusum. It is his plan to make his son a man, not a donkey like himself. He speaks about Balram: "My whole life, I have been treated like a donkey. All I want is that one son of mine—at least one—should live like a man" (30). What Balram is today is because of his father who never bowed before anyone. He makes himself different from the other students in the school and the school inspector compliments him saying that he is "an intelligent, honest, vivacious fellow in this crowd of thugs and idiots". He also tags him as the white tiger in this jungle. His initial career as a student shows that he is not born to be caged in the coop. Though he does not read much poetry, he appreciates four Muslim poets. He is fond of Iqbal who has written about slaves: *"They remain slaves because they can't see what is beautiful in this world"* (40). Even in his boyhood, he has the capability of seeing what is beautiful in the world. This capability makes one thing clear—that he will not lead a life of slave forever. Somehow he gathers courage and enters the Black Fort which makes him see his little Laxmangarh. He spits in the direction of the village. This spitting is the spitting on the traditional values which he rejects. He feels that traditional values become a coop and never let the man come out.

Balram Halwai is a split personality that oscillates between love and hate. He himself does not know when his hatred turns into love and love into hatred. He himself generalises when he says: "no servant can ever tell what the motives of his heart are" (187). He looks after his master Mr Ashok when Pinky Madam leaves him. He wipes the vomit from his lips and speaks soothing words to him. At one point he realises that his real feelings for his master give way to the selfishness. He interrogates himself: "Do we loathe our masters behind a façade of love—or do we love them behind a façade of loathing?" (187) but does not come to any conclusion. He is a mystery to himself because of the rooster coop in which he is. He does not think of marriage which will result in children who will be asses like him for carrying "rubble around for the rich" (193). He is a human being and so wishes to be treated like a human being. The problem arises when animals are treated as human beings and human beings animals. His simple philosophy is: "Let animals live like animals; let humans live like humans. That's my whole philosophy in a sentence" (276). It is the Rooster Coop that makes human beings animals. To materialise his philosophy he breaks the coop by murdering his master Mr Ashok and then leads a life of a free man.

No doubt, Balram breaks the coop in spite of the various adverse circumstances that are faced by him. He is mentally tortured by his own apprehensiveness. He recalls the Buffalo's treatment to the family of his servant. Now, his mind's eye sees a buffalo pulling the cart. The buffalo seems to warn him about his family and the consequence of the action that he is about to take. Though it is a kind of nightmare, he seems to hear that his brother Kishan was beaten to death, aunt Luttu was raped and granny Kusum was kicked to death. He sees the cart "full of dead skinned faces" which are the faces of his family members. The family makes him think of his action which proves to be a rooster coop. He becomes indecisive but he is determined to come out of the coop and so does not care for the family. He knows that only a man who is "prepared to see his family destroyed—hunted, beaten, and burned alive by the masters—can break out of the coop" and for this he must not be a "normal human being, but a freak, a pervert of nature" (177). He can change the circumstances in his favour. The couplet: *"I was looking for the key for years / But the door was always open"* (267) makes him relaxed to the extent that he goes to sleep. He has now no master as he is his own master.

The murder of Mr Ashok makes Balram free from the stigma of slavery. With the red bag full of money, he goes to Bangalore where he wishes to settle. He goes to meet a Toyota Qualis dealer and asks him for his cars on rent. Initially he does not say that he needs his cars on rent but the mentality of being a servant makes him utter that he wants to drive his car. Such a statement makes the dealer confused. But, soon, he gathers himself and says that he needs car on rent. He states: "Once a servant, always a servant: the instinct is always there, inside you, somewhere near the base of your spine. I pinched my left palm. I smiled as I held it pinched and said—in a deep, gruff voice, 'I want to *rent* your cars' (299). Now he becomes from "a driver to a master" to "a master of drivers" and treats his employees professionally. He does not have any friendship with them because friendship is dangerous for a white tiger. He translates his philosophy of treating humans as humans and animals as animals. It gives really pleasure to the servant who even for a minute feels that he is not a servant after all. It is surprising that Balram, the lover of freedom, talks of slavery. He opposes the coop and breaks it but why is he interested in marriage? What is it that makes him announce that he is ready to have children? Why does he wish to have children? Does he wish for children without marriage because marriage is a rooster coop? He is against the institution of marriage. Why he wishes to have children is a question mark. But, one thing that he makes clear "the Rooster Coop needs people like me to break out of it. It needs masters like Mr Ashok—who, for all his numerous virtues, was not much of a master- to be weeded out, and exceptional servants like me to replace them" (320). He feels himself victorious and utters aloud: *"I've made it! I've broken out of the coop"* (320)!

One thing that differentiates him from others is that he recognises what is beautiful in the world and this very recognizance gives him the power to be free. No doubt, he finds himself surrounded by circumstances all around but in the end, he does not lose courage and changes the circumstances in his favour.

Many men remain in the coop because of adverse circumstances which become so strong that they fail to break the bars of the coop. But, Balram is not made of such stuff. He is a man of iron will that gives him strength enough to fight against the odds. Circumstances bow down and open the door of the coop for him. Yes, it is true that Aravind Adiga has given Balram Halwai the mantra of coming out of the coop and its chanting gives him inner strength that breaks all the chains of slavery. But, what about the coop of Marxism in which the creator of Balram is himself in? Will he come out of it—is still debatable. Does he have the inner strength to tolerate the value of religion in human life? Adiga's metaphor of the rooster coop has given mental food to the intellectual world that interprets in its own way. But, the interpretations are theirs only, not of Adiga. What the interpretation of Adiga is still as ambiguous as his protagonist Balram Halwai who considers one murder a necessary requirement for being a free man.

WORK CITED

Adiga, Aravind. *The White Tiger*. New Delhi: HarperCollins, 2008. **Print.**

9

The Poor Bastards: The Subalterns

> These poor bastards had come from the Darkness to Delhi to find some light—but they were still in the darkness. (138)

The rich cannot live without the poor. The rich always wish them to be poor, otherwise who will work for them?. As long as the monster capital is there, it will create a gulf and separate the two, showing them the two different paths which never meet each other.

Yeats's line "Intellectual hatred is the worst" applies to no one better than Aravind Adiga who makes his protagonist Balram Halwai write such abusive words in the letter meant for the Chinese Premier. The questions: "How can *The White Tiger* be a *dalit* text? How can Balram Halwai a messiah for the lower caste and the economically weaker exploited class known as *dalit* or subaltern?" are still debatable. Has Adiga made the subaltern speak? If yes, is the way that he has adopted right?

'Dalit' is a much contested term because of its various interpretations and the way that it gives birth to the tug of war between the centre and the periphery. Questions like "What is the parameter for being *dalit*? Is it caste? Is it backwardness? Is it financial condition?" are either unanswered or answered differently by different types of people. If 'exploitation' is the criteria for being a *dalit*, it includes all. Is the scheduled caste the only class that is exploited? Are the other castes or classes not exploited and oppressed? Other castes, if they are exploited and oppressed also claim to being *dalits*. If taken from the narrow view, *dalit* literature is concerned only with the scheduled caste and scheduled tribes but from the macro level it includes other castes as well. In *The White Tiger*, it seems that Adiga is dishing out the communist ideology in the disguise of *dalitism*. He has not mentioned the very touchstones that make any text a *dalit* text. Probably, he does not wish to confine *dalit* literature to self-pity, a crisis for identity, an invocation to Dr. Ambedkar, a protest or open revolt against the touchables. But, it is not such as Adiga seems to propound through Balram Halwai who thinks himself the emancipator of many poor people whom he saves from ending up "in a mound of indistinguishable bodies that will rot in the black mud of Mother Ganga" (318).

The White Tiger is a challenge to the *varna* system which has placed *shudras* to the lower strata. Is the *varna* system according to *karma* or caste? Is it not misrepresentation to make out the meaning according to one's wish?

When India got freedom in 1947, the caste system shattered because of the animals in man who broke the cages. The zoo law gave place to the jungle law. Balram states:

> And then, thanks to all those politicians in Delhi, on the fifteenth of August, 1947—the day the British left—the cages had been let open; and the animals had attacked and ripped each other apart and jungle law replaced zoo law. Those that were the most ferocious, the hungriest, had eaten everyone else up, and grown big bellies. That was all that counted now, the size of your belly. It didn't matter whether you were a woman, or a Muslim, or an untouchable: anyone with a belly could rise up. (64)
>
> To sum up—in the old days there were one thousand castes and destinies in India. These days, there are just two castes: Men with Big Bellies, and Men with Small Bellies.
>
> And only two destinies: eat—or get eaten up. (64)

In the wake of freedom, a new parameter in the form of belly emerged in determining the caste. Out of thousand castes, only two castes—Men with Big Bellies and Men with Small Bellies—are prevalent. But, even then, the mental set-up is still a slave to the *varna* system. Often, it is the caste that makes one guess about the personality of the other person. Halwai, the caste of Balram, becomes responsible for making the destiny. When anyone hears the name Halwai he guesses that the Halwai knows how to prepare sweets. *"Ah, they're Halwais, making sweets and tea is in their blood"* (63). If he is a Halwai, his father must also own a sweet-shop. But, to the contrary, his father pulls a rickshaw. He tells the Stork that he belongs to the Halwai caste. The Stork asks whether Halwai is "a top caste or bottom caste" but he will not mind having a low caste employee because all other employees belong to the high caste. Other activities also result from this caste factor. A halwai is not supposed to drink alcohol. He is expected to cook and also make sweets like *gulab jamuns, laddoos*. Even when he goes to learn driving, the caste comes on the way as a halwai is not expected to drive a car. The old driver wonders: "You make sweets. How can you learn to drive" (56)? For him, it is caste that determines a profession. Driving is meant for Muslims, Rajputs, Sikhs, not for a halwai. He tells Balram: "Mastering a car'—he moved the stick of an invisible gearbox—'it's like taming a wild stallion—only a boy from the warrior castes can manage that. You need to have aggression in your blood. Muslims, Rajputs, Sikhs—they're fighters, they can become drivers. You think sweet-makers can last long in fourth gear?' (56) But, later on, Balram breaks this illusion and emerges as a surprise pack for the old driver. He proves that it is not caste that determines a profession but will power and determination.

The protagonist Halwai loves freedom and wishes to be free but the problem with the Indian people is that they "don't understand the value of freedom" (117). He respects the Chinese because they are "great lovers of freedom and individual liberty" and admires their spirit of freedom though the British tried their best to make them slaves. It is the love for freedom in him that he has broken the tag of a servant. He calls himself "a half-baked Indian" and expresses his pain over the fact that India is full of half-baked people like him. People like him remain half-baked as they are not allowed to complete their schooling. He asks the Chinese Premier:

> Open our skulls, look in with a penlight, and you'll find an odd museum of ideas: sentences of history or mathematics remembered from school textbooks, sentences about politics read in a newspaper while waiting for someone to come to an office, triangles and pyramids seen on the torn pages of the old geometry textbooks which every tea shop in this country uses to wrap its snacks in, bits of All Indian Radio news bulletins, things that drop into your mind, like lizards from the ceiling, in the half-hour before falling asleep—all these ideas, half formed and half digested and half correct, mix up with other half-cooked ideas in your head, and I guess these half-formed ideas bugger one another, and make more half-formed ideas, and this is what you act on and live with. (10-11)

This is not the case of only Balram but of many Balrams who are taken out of the school for the various reasons and, thus, remain devoid of proper education. Though he is now in Bangalore and settled as an entrepreneur, the reality is that he was "born and raised in Darkness" (14). As a student in the school, he differentiates himself from other students and gets the title of the white tiger—the rarest of rare—from the inspector who promises to write to Patna for his scholarship. He says to Balram: "You need to go to a real school—somewhere far away from here. You need a real uniform, and a real education" (35). But, on account of the loan that was taken from the Stork for the marriage, every member has to go to work as a bonded labour. He has to leave the school for "Working in a tea shop. Smashing coals. Wiping tables" (38). The thing that makes him different from others is that he is not born to be a servant forever. As he is ambitious to be free and do something different, he learns driving and becomes a chauffeur to Mr Ashok and Pinky Madam. When he comes to the village, he reaches the top of the Black Fort where earlier he used to fear even to enter. From there, he sees all the things related to his village Laxmangarh—"the temple tower, the market, line of sewage, the landlords' mansions" (42) and his own house with the water buffalo. He spits again and again towards his village. This spitting shows the spitting over the old traditions and fetters that chained him. What he needs is to be free from any kind of slavery. His determination to be against slavery makes him emotionless to the extent that he murders his master and steals the red bag with the money.

The high caste people do not leave any occasion for exploitation which is in their blood. The Stork family exploits servants emotionally and physically. They call a servant a member of the family but do not treat him as such. When Balram goes for the job of a chauffeur, the Stork is in his favour not because he drives well but because he is young and can be exploited for the next thirty or thirty-five years. He shares with his sons: "Catch'em young, and you can keep 'em for life. A driver in his forties, you get, what, twenty years of service, then his eyes fail. This fellow will last thirty, thirty-five years. His teeth are solid, he's got his hair, he's in good shape" (66). Servants are not servants but commodities at the disposal of the high castes.

Ram Bahadur has been serving the family for the last thirty years. Besides being the guard, he performs other activities as well. Mr Ashok tells Pinky Madam that it is almost impossible to find someone like Ram Bahadur who can bring tea and biscuits to the masters who are in bed. Mr Mukesh humiliates Balram for a rupee when he asks him to look for it on the floor though his brother Mr Ashok asks him not to do so as one rupee is immaterial to them when they have spent millions of rupees in bribery.

When Balram fails to find out a rupee, he takes out one rupee from his pocket and gives it to Mr Mukesh who feels a sigh of relief. It is not the only case, he has to bear the torture, insult and humiliation from the hands of Pinky Madam who makes fun of him for mispronouncing words like Maal and Pizza. He feels humiliated to the extent that he blames his father for not teaching him how to brush. He cries: "Why had my father never told me not to scratch my groin? Why had my father never taught me to brush my teeth in milky foam? Why had he raised me to live like an animal? Why do all the poor live amid such filth, such ugliness" (151)?

The people belonging to the upper caste exploit their servants emotionally and make them ready to admit the crimes which they have not committed. It happens with Balram who is forced to go to jail for the crime that was committed by Pinky Madam. Pinky Madam in a drunkard state drives and hits a boy but Balram is made to take the crime on himself. He realises that no doubt, people like him have left the village but the reality is that today "the master still own us, body, soul, and arse" (170). They appreciate the servant and tag them as "the perfect servant". A servant is expected to save the honour of the family of his master. When Pinky Madam leaves Mr Ashok, he does not tell any driver the truth and, hence, remains "loyal to the last" (183). But, the case of hit-and-run makes him re-think and re-evaluate the relationship. A servant keeps the motives of his heart confined to him. The fear of losing his job makes him pray in the temple that "Pinky Madam and Mr Ashok should be reunited and given a long and happy life together in Delhi" (187). It happens with the servants that they themselves do not know when they hate or love their masters. Balram is also not sure when he says: "Do we loathe our masters behind a façade of love—or do we love them behind a façade of loathing? We are made mysteries to ourselves by the Rooster Coop we are locked in" (187). The lava in the form of anger mixed with this mystery erupts from the volcano which propels him to cheat his master. As he is not a born servant, he thinks of changing his status and for this he himself develops evils of his master. It is Delhi that corrupts Mr Ashok and "once the master of the Honda City becomes corrupted, how can the driver stay innocent" (197). The more he cheats his master, the more enraged he feels. He shares with the Chinese Premier:

> Over the next two weeks, I did things I am still ashamed to admit. I cheated my employer. I siphoned his petrol; I took his car to a corrupt mechanic who billed him for work that was not necessary; and three times, while driving back to Buckingham B, I picked up a paying customer.
>
> The strangest thing was that each time I looked at the cash I had made by cheating him, instead of guilt, what did I feel?
>
> Rage.
>
> The more I stole from him, the more I realised how much he had stolen from me.

> To go back to the analogy I used when describing Indian politics to you earlier, I was growing a belly at last. (230)

He makes up his mind not to remain a servant anymore and this determination makes him declare before Vitiligo-Lips: "I am my own master" (231).

The financially weaker people who fail even to get employment in the village come to the cities in the hope of better opportunities that will bring light into their lives but unfortunately they are more exploited than ever and are left in darkness amidst light. This is the miserable condition of the *dalits,* particularly economically weak ones who do not have even enough to earn bread for their livelihood. Mark the pitiable condition of the poor wretched:

> Thousands of people live on the sides of the road in Delhi. They have come from the Darkness too—you can tell by their thin bodies, filthy faces, by the animal-like way they live under the huge bridges and overpasses, making fires and washing and taking lice out of their hair while the cars roar past them. These homeless people are a particular problem for drivers. They never wait for a red light—simply dashing across the road on impulse. (120)

These are the poor people who live in the darkness but give light to the rich people who think that they are merely commodities which can be purchased. They are not treated as human beings because they have nothing substantial except their labours. The rich do not even pay the proper amount for their labour. A driver is not a driver but a servant who is expected to perform all the activities which are commanded by his master. These poor people who come to the city do not have roofs over their heads and remain devoid of the basic amenities required for the minimum level of living. They prepare roofs for the rich but themselves remain roofless. They build "homes for the rich" but live "in tents covered with blue tarpaulin sheets" (260). They are forced to lead a life of deprivation and humiliation.

Pinky Madam in her drunkard state hits a child. No case is reported because the sufferer has no approach and, hence, remains far away from the rule of justice. Slavery is written large on their faces. They are no better than cockroaches which see others being crushed and do nothing because of their hopelessness. Light becomes illusion for them. While remaining in the light, their own lives remain in darkness.

Balram Halwai is not destined to remain poor and, in the end, succeeds in getting the job of a chauffeur. Even Delhi is two cities—inside and outside. It is the car that makes the people safe from pollution while the people on the footpath absorb the pollution and become victims of diseases. Balram who drives the car feels that he is in the right city. But, at the subconscious level, he imagines that if his father had been alive he would have been "sitting on that pavement, cooking some rice gruel for dinner, and getting ready to lie and sleep under a streetlamp" (138). He cannot help himself in finding the features of his father in some beggar lying there. Poverty is itself a disease which does not allow a man to enter a mall. The cry: "Am I not a human being too?" (148) seems to be the cry of every *dalit*.

The rich are few while the poor are many. Does it not sound strange that "so few owed so much to so many" (175)? It is the handful of rich people dominating over the poor who are "as strong, as talent, as intelligent in every way" but still remain in "perpetual servitude" (176) which is too strong to break in spite of the key of emancipation in their hands. It is on account of the rooster coop that works from inside as well as outside. The coop may be in the form of the family system or in the form of circumstances. They believe that circumstances determine man, not man circumstances. One who believes in one's power of changing circumstances according to one's desire is eligible to come out of the rooster coop. Almost all the *dalits* are in the rooster coop—the coop of caste, the coop of circumstances, the coop of poverty or any other created by the rich to imprison them. In spite of their desire to come out, they fail to do so. The only thing that can provide them a minimum level of living is their union which is always broken by the hammer of capitalism. This union can be brought by Baba Ambedkar's formula that recommends education first so that the *dalits* may recognise the strength of organisation, and the moment they recognise this strength, their agitation can bring the rich to the back foot.

Politics is also responsible for the miserable condition of the *dalits* to a great extent. The breads of politics are baked in the name of *dalits'* emancipation. India is a democratic country where everyone has the right to vote. But, it is in name only. The reality is that such poor people remain devoid of voting rights as their votes are already purchased or manipulated by the dominating power. Balram presents the scene when he was enrolled in the voter list. Ironically he says: "I had to be eighteen. All of us in the tea shop had to be eighteen, the legal age to vote. There was an election coming up, and the tea shop owner had already sold us" (97). It is also a sad fact that when any pro-*dalit* government gets power, it does not remain *a dalit* government. When a dalit gets power and wealth he becomes a man of repute and respect. The Great Socialist insults Mr Mukesh when he asks him to hold the spittoon in which he spits three times. This activity on the part of the Great Socialist makes him red with shame. Balram witnesses the scene and inwardly enjoys when he sees the Mongoose being humiliated. Humiliation of the upper caste by the Great Socialist wins the heart of the *dalits* who keep on voting for him so that he may remain in power. When a *dalit* gets power he expects respect from a Brahmin. He loves to tease the non-*dalits* because it gives him pleasure "better than an erection" (271). Where the feeling for *dalits* disappears remains a mystery. Balram's hero is Vijay who, being an opportunist, continues to change his position. His journey from a bus conductor via politics to public service is a source of inspiration for Balram. It is the magic of politics that makes even the Stork, the landlord, bow down before Vijay, the pigherd's son.

No respectable father longs for a life of insult and humiliation for his children. Balram's father Vikram Halwai, in spite of being a rickshaw-puller, is in favour of education. When he comes to know that his son has come from the school, he yells at Kusum and says that "Munna *must* read and write" (28) while she asks him to "put him to work in the tea shop and let him make some money" (28). But, his father wishes that his son "should live like a man" (30). No doubt, he is a dropout but believes in education and so continues to learn through eavesdropping. He overhears the conversations and increases his knowledge. While driving the car, he keeps his ears open to the conversation of Mr Ashok and Pinky Madam who chat "about life, about India, about America—and a bit of English too" (47). He confesses that he is "not an original thinker" but "an original *listener*" (47). He proves himself to be the best servant for Mr Ashok and Pinky Madam. When he drives the car with his master and mistress, he feels like Hanuman carrying Rama and Sita.

It sounds ridiculous that animals are treated as human beings and human beings as animals. The rich like to have puppies that are not only treated as human beings but also considered more valuable than the poor bastards. In the Stork family there are two white pomeranians that are being treated as human beings. Balram says: "There were two white Pomeranians in the house—Cuddles and Puddles. The rich expect their dogs to be treated like humans, you see—they expect their dogs to be pampered, and walked, and petted, and even washed" (78). When he takes them out the Nepali guard asks him not to "pull the chain so hard" because "they are more worth" (78) than he is.

The rich make a show of love to the poor while the reality is that they exploit them and do not give what they deserve. Mr Ashok praises Balram because he never asks for money like other drivers. He convinces him that he will take care of the wedding expenses. First he takes out a thousand-rupee note but in the end gives him only a hundred-rupee note. This is the help that he offers making Balram realise that he will take care of everything. As he is lost in the thinking process, he thinks that this master will not hesitate even in fucking his wife in the name of help. "We'll even fuck your wife for you, Balram" (261). He realises his miserable condition and plans about how to come out from such slavery. He recites a couplet from Iqbal. "*I was looking for the key for years / But the door was always open*" (267). Again a conflict between God and the

Devil occurs in his mind. God makes the Devil realise that he is powerful and huge and asks him to become his servant. This is the same case with the landlords or capitalists who think themselves as gods and so do their best in making the poor their servants. God asks the little man: *"Isn't it all wonderful? Isn't it all grand? Aren't you grateful to be my servant"* (88)? Again the voice of God seems to be the voice of the capitalist or the landlord. The little man is none other than the reflection of Balram who has gathered lava in him against the world of the rich. The spitting of the little man in khaki makes Balram more determined than ever.

> And then I see this small black man in the wet khaki uniform start to shake, as if he has gone mad with anger, before delivering to the Almighty a gesture of thanks for having created the world this particular way, instead of all the other ways it could have been created.
>
> I see the little man in the khaki uniform *spitting* at God again and again, as I watch the black blades of the midget fan slice the light from the chandelier again and again. (88)

When he sees the red bag with seven hundred thousand rupees, he thinks that it belongs to the people like him. He murders Mr Ashok, takes the bag and becomes free. He takes the cars on rent and, later, develops his business to such an extent that he becomes a rich entrepreneur whose motive is to take technology forward. He opines that he has given voice to the poor bastard by setting an example. He feels that he is "a part of all that is changing this country" and has got success "in the struggle that every poor man here should be making –the struggle not to take the lashes your father took, not to end up in a mound of indistinguishable bodies that will rot in the black mud of Mother Ganga" (318). He has come out of the coop and for this he murders his master but he thinks that the murder was an essential requirement for "the change to be a man" (318). His justification of the murder of his master seems ridiculous. His case offers the tip for being a man. Murder and be a man. It may be a sound advice for people like Balram. But, all the *dalits* are not Balram and can never be so destructive in their action and thought. The way he shows to the subalterns is the way that leads to hell, not heaven.

Baba Ambedkar gives the mantra of struggle for the emancipation of *dalits*. He never suggests the means of agitation at first attempt but rather advocates education which will be the cementing force in organising all under one roof. Then, the step of agitation will become effective in liberating them from exploitation and oppression. Here, Adiga has given an unusual mantra to Halwai for his emancipation and also the people like him. Serve, Slay and then Steal. What will happen if all the subalterns follow Balram and chant the mantra? Certainly, it is not genuine. Killing one another will result in the emancipation of the humanity—the emancipation in the form of extinction of the human species. Peace will give way to anarchy that will make a havoc dance of slaughter. Under such mantra the future of the *dalit* or rather human beings is beyond imagination. The question arises here if Adiga is a true supporter of the *dalit*. Does he not have any other way or mantra for the *dalits'* struggle? Is murder of the master the only way left for the servant for taking the place of master? It seems absurd that one whose philosophy is: "Let animals live like animals; let humans live like humans (276)" suggests one murder in life to be a man. How can animals live like animals and humans like humans when humans become animals? Balram feels proud of himself that he has succeeded in breaking the coop and providing the facilities for the poor to become man. He is rather professional, not the human in the treatment of his employees. It is all right that he does not treat his employees like servants and also does not "slap or bully, or mock anyone" but when he says: "when the work is done I kick them out of the office: no chitchat, no cup of coffee. A White Tiger keeps no friends" (302), his claim becomes weak. He does not call his employees servants because he speaks little. What his tongue cannot do is performed by his leg that kicks the employees as soon as the work is over. How can he be an exploiter when he himself is against it? Who will judge? Very proudly, he thinks of himself as an icon for improving life-standard. He states: "If they notice the way I talk, the way I dress, the way I keep things clean, they'll go up in life. If they don't, they'll be drivers all their lives. I leave the choice up to them" (302).

Balram suggests the way to his employers for rising to the status by following his way of talking, dressing, keeping things clean. What will happen if the drivers follow his example? Is there any guarantee if an ambitious driver may murder Balram Halwai and become the master—the driver of drivers? 'Circumstances make man' gives place to 'man makes circumstances' for an ambitious man. What Balram speaks today will be spoken tomorrow by a more powerful white tiger. "Once I was a driver to a master, but now I am a master of drivers" (302). The story of murder will continue.

A *dalit* text voices *dalits* and their identity protesting against the images, language and symbols advocated by the higher caste in favour of their own idioms and symbols. But, when a *dalit* himself speaks the language of the higher caste and follows their way of life, what will be the difference? Not to talk of language, even the name of higher caste is adopted by the protagonist. Balram Halwai becomes Ashok Sharma in the end of the novel.

Today Halwai is what Ashok Sharma was. Whose victory? Whose emancipation? Whose voice? Is Balram Halwai subaltern in the disguise of Ashok Sharma? Does he not seem to be embracing capitalism? It is capitalism that exploits the poor through a new kind of feudalism? Though he advocates communism, he is tempted by the pleasure of capitalism. Everything is sale for him. The red bag that makes him red petticoats available is responsible for his transformation not from a servant to a master but a human being into a monster that never hesitates in shedding red blood. He does yoga which makes him survive, otherwise he would have no peace of mind. He sends Dharam to the English school where he learns the Western ways that prepare a ground for sowing the seeds of slavery. The way of his protest against the exploitation is not sound as it will lead society on the path of anarchy.

Adiga's Balram does not translate into action what he claims to be. Does he voice *dalits* or himself become a non-*dalit* through the magic of red bag and then exploit *the dalits*? Why does he use the name of Ashok Sharma, his master? His disguise as Brahmin Ashok Sharma puts a full stop to his claim to being a messiah for the *dalits*. How can he forget the name of Ambedkar whose ideals are the source of inspiration for all the *dalits*? The mantra of struggle from Dr. Ambedkar, the magic of serenity from Lord Buddha, the value of education from Jyotiba Phule and the force of protest from Periyar are the four ingredients which prepare an anti-dote, named, 'Dalit literature' for the affirmation of the *dalit* identity against the *brahminic* syndrome. Aravind Adiga's text *The White Tiger* does not have these ingredients and, hence, cannot be called a *dalit* text on the plea that it has Balram Halwai—a *dalit* protagonist for whom the poor people are bastards.

WORK CITED

Adiga, Aravind. *The White Tiger*. New Delhi: HarperCollins, 2008. **Print.**

10

The Freudian Lava

It is a fashion to peep into the text through the Freudian specs that often reveal some aspects of personality which one never expects. Whatever a man does has some connection with the unconscious mind. The mind of childhood is the best receptor of observations and feelings which, though remaining repressed because of certain circumstances, appear at a later stage in adulthood. If studied from this point of view, Aravind Adiga's *The White Tiger* is a psychological novel. It will be an exciting as well as shaking experience to go into the depth of the mind in order to know its inner working and the impressions that lie underneath somewhere.

The family is responsible for making or marring the personality of a child. The great role is played by the parents—in most cases either by the mother or the father. The case of Balram Halwai is not different because both father and mother have shaped his personality. No doubt, his mother is no more and Balram sees her cremation with his own eyes at the bank of the river Ganga. Though it seems ridiculous to state that he is a victim of the Oedipus complex, there is a grain of truth in it. He is shocked at her death and the way of cremating her makes him cry within. She is wrapped in a saffron silk cloth though she never wore such a fine thing when she was alive. The cremation in a grand manner makes him believe that "her life must have been miserable" and to some extent it is true because his family was "guilty about something" (16). The guilt from the granny Kusum shows that "She was a good, quiet girl the day she came to our home" (17) but this praise does not convince Balram who does not wish for any fight on this issue though he registers his opposition through shaking her hand off his face. Mark the excerpt for the brave spirit of Balram's mother even after death:

> As the fire ate away the satin, a pale foot jerked out, like a living thing; the toes, which were melting in the heat, began to curl up, offering resistance to what was being done to them. Kusum shoved the foot into the fire, but it would not burn. My heart began to race. My mother wasn't going to let them destroy her. (17)

Even the dead mother resists the fire through her toes and it seems that her body does not wish to be destroyed in spite of the efforts of Granny who shoves her foot into it. The oozing of the black mud because of the waves from the shore does not let the body burn properly. He reflects over the mud, the toes and dog while observing the scene of cremation.

> This mud was holding her back: this big, swelling mound of black ooze. She was trying to fight the black mud: her toes were flexed and resisting; but the mud was sucking her in, sucking her in. It was so thick, and more of it was being created every moment as the river washed into the *ghat*. Soon she would become part of the black mound and the pale-skinned dog would start licking her. (17-18)

Often it is seen that the unburnt part of the dead body is released into the Ganga. He fears and imagines that the same will happen to him when he will be brought for cremation. Somehow he develops a hatred for the river Ganga, whether it is due to the mud that stops the toes from burning or the mother herself that the Ganga took in her embrace through, fire. He is so much obsessed with the Ganga that he faints and never goes there later. For him, the Ganga is not the river of life but the black river—the river of death. But, about his mother he thinks good and imagines that she might have gone to heaven. He thinks: "In the distance, an island of white sand glistened in the sunlight, and boats full of people were heading to that island. I wondered if my mother's soul had flown there, to that shining place in the river" (17). But, he does not come out of the shock that continues to torture him. At the end of the novel, he has "a vision of a pale, stiff foot pushing through a fire" (193) and to get over this shocking vision that reminds him of his mother he sits in the lotus position and does yoga chanting 'Om' again and again. The scene of his mother's toes at the bank of the Ganga haunts him to the extent that even when he thinks of murder, he becomes conscious of the victim's toes. He states:

> Here's a strange fact: murder a man, and you feel responsible for his life—possessive, even. You know more about him than his father and mother; they knew his foetus, but you know his corpse. Only you can complete the story of his life only you know why his body has to be pushed into the fire before its time, and why his toes curl up and fight for another hour on earth. (46-47)

One thing is obvious—that Balram loves his mother and wishes to be what she expected from him. Kusum had been against her because of her spirit of freedom and individuality. She would go to the Fort in order to know the mystery. Her longing for exploring the Fort shows her adventurous spirit. This is what Balram has. When he goes to the Fort with the intention of going in, the granny Kusum finds him and complains to his father Vikram Halwai. She compares his actions with his mother's.

> One day Kusum found out about me and the fort. She followed me all the way form our home to the pond with the stones, and saw what I was doing. That night she told my father, 'He just stood here gaping at the fort—just the way his mother used to. He is going to come to nothing good in life, I'll tell you that right now.' (41)

What type of a lady Balram's mother was can be guessed from Kusum's statement. Later, when Balram becomes a chauffeur to the Stork family and gets a chance to go to Delhi, Kishan who comes to meet him expresses joy at the news. He shares his mother's prophecy that her son would one day come out of darkness and enter the light in order to make a good future. Kishan says: "Someone in his family was going to make it out of the Darkness and into New Delhi! It's just like our mother always said. She knew you were going to make it" (111). The remark of Kishan clearly shows the wishes of the mother and the dream which she had for her sons. Hence, the mother is ever present in his unconsciousness that comes to consciousness via preconscious state of mind.

The death of his mother makes him alone to the extent that he searches for her presence in every woman but unfortunately does not find her anywhere. He becomes a morally unrestrained person and enjoys sex. The lizard is present in his psyche that appears again and again without his knowledge in spite of having the chandelier everywhere in his prosperous life. He is so much obsessed with his mother that later when he fails to find inner satisfaction from the purchased fair bodies, he thinks that he is "ready to have children" (321) so that he may have a permanent life member who will look after him well. Kusum calls Balram a coward because of his fear of the lizard. He, no doubt, loves animals but the lizard makes him "turn into a girl" (28) and freezes his blood. He faints the second time in his life when the boys bring a lizard close to his face to frighten him. He faints for the first time when he imagines his own death and the cremation on the bank of the river Ganga like his mother whose toes remained unburnt. Kusum also takes an advantage of Balram's fear to keep him away from the Black Fort, the fort that reminds her of his mother. The lizard becomes the symbol of evil that is ever present in him. What it needs is a wall to move on. Balram forcibly encroaches upon Mr Ashok's wall by murdering him and appears to be a fair man in the light of the chandelier that makes the lizard disappear but to think that it has gone away forever is foolishness. Ashok's father loved chandeliers and "wanted to put one up in the bathroom here" (83). Pinky Madam does not like the chandelier in the old mansion and thinks that "it's a bit tacky" as she does not expect the light in India, the only right that the West has. When Ashok's father loves chandeliers, why will he not like to have them when "they keep the lizards away from this room" (117)? It is the chandelier that gives the feel of freedom and even then "people don't buy chandeliers all the time, and put them up everywhere" (117). He thinks that chandeliers are his family members and, hence, keeps them in the drawing room and also in toilet, "the only toilet in Bangalore with a chandelier" (117).

What Balram is today is what his father Vikram Halwai has made him. But, his father, if he had been alive, would have never suggested to him to murder his master. He calls his father *Mr* Vikram Halwai to offer his regards to a man who, in spite of being poor, was "a man of honour and courage" and he had never been here "under this chandelier, if not for his guidance" (23). Whenever he sees his father, he finds him "shirtless, usually alone, drinking tea and thinking" (24). He never crouched but "chose to fight" (27). He may have been a rickshaw-puller but never expected his son to be so. He wishes to see his son educated and so sends him to school.

Balram differentiates himself from other students and gets the title of the white tiger from the school inspector. The day his father comes to know that Munna has come from school, he yells at Kusum who lets him know about his son's cowardice regarding the lizard. The old man goes to the school where he takes the lizard in his hand, smashes its neck and stamps its head out of anger. He does it to remove the fear from the mind of Balram whom he wishes to see as a brave man. He does not wish for him the life of a donkey that he himself is leading but wants that his son "should live like a man" (30). The smashing of the neck is imprinted on Balram's psyche somewhere which comes forcibly when he smashes the neck of Mr Ashok besides injuring the head.

He recalls the death of his father from tuberculosis which in the advanced stage makes him spit blood. When he takes his father to the hospital, he washes his mouth with water from the river but "the water was so polluted that it made him spit more blood" (48). He sees the death of his father with his eyes and later kills his own employer Mr Ashok, "a kind of second father" with his own hands. This murder makes him "a virtual mass murderer" (45) because it results in the probable death of all his family members. One thing in this murder is similar and certainly it is the result of the unconscious mind that becomes conscious through the preconscious. As a boy, Balram would play with his father. Mark the excerpt:

> I would come to him, and play around with him, by climbing his back, and passing my palm over his forehead—over his eyes—over his nose—and down to his neck, to the little depression at the pit of his neck. I would let my finger linger there—it still is my favourite part of the human body. (26)

He could control his father and stop his breathing touching the pit of the neck with the pressure of his finger. He follows the same technique while killing Mr Ashok whom, after striking his head with the bottle, pierces his neck to the extent that "his lifeblood spurted into his eyes" (286) making the slavery in him blind in paving the way to his freedom. The blood that comes out from the neck is the anger that he repressed when he saw his father spitting blood through his mouth. But, the killing of Mr Ashok is better and easier than the death of his father. The sentence: "But then tuberculosis is a worse way to go than this, I assure you" (286) that he speaks just after killing makes it clear that he has the image of his father in mind and somewhere he is releasing his anger and trying to be a man which his father expected from him. No doubt, he loves his father but sometimes shows his anger at him because of not teaching him the civilised way of life. Pinky Madam mocks at him for his dirty teeth and his habit of scratching his groin. Mark the excerpt for his repressed anger that comes out because of Pinky Madam who carves out an outlet for his feelings:

> Why had my father never told me not to scratch my groin? Why had my father never taught me to brush my teeth in

> milky foam? Why had he raised me to live like an animal? Why do all the poor live amid such filth, such ugliness?
>
> Brush. Brush. Spit.
>
> Brush. Brush. Spit.
>
> If only a man could spit his past out so easily. (151)

He feels inferior, insulted and humiliated before her. He holds his father responsible for not telling him that scratching the groin is not a civilised sign. He brushes his teeth to whiten them and wishes that he could spit his past. It is quite psychological that a child holds his father responsible for not teaching certain things, the failure of which make him uncivilised. What Balram does here is not new as he is releasing his anger not on his father, rather on the things which became responsible for the insult. Mark the excerpt that shows the abusive and insulting words used by Pinky Madam:

> 'You're a filthy! Look at you, look at your teeth, look at your clothes! There's red *paan* all over you teeth, and there are red spots on your shirt. It's disgusting! Get out—clean up the mess you've made in the kitchen and get out.' (146)

Such insulting remarks can make anyone angry. It becomes easy to digest the insulting words spoken by the person of the same sex but to hear from the opposite sex develops an anger that gives birth to an inferiority complex and it becomes almost impossible to forget the tart remarks. Hence, the man searches for a medium to level the insult. Sometimes he releases the anger with his close relative whom he thinks to be his own. He cannot be violent at the time because of his status of being a servant and, so, releases his anger by recalling the dead father and holding him responsible for not teaching the things mentioned by Pinky Madam.

Pinky's insulting behaviour breaks him while the insult from the hands of Mr Mukesh, the Mongoose, makes him laugh arousing pity towards his childish behaviour. A millionaire who bribes with lakhs of rupees shows his concern for a rupee to the extent that its loss makes him restless. He remains troubled and cries for a rupee till he gets it. Mukesh asks Balram to search for a rupee. Balram initially feels insulted when Mukesh forces him to search for the lost one-rupee coin. Mr Ashok favours Balram and asks Mukesh to let it go. Why does he care for a rupee when they are doling out million of rupees as bribe to politicians? Even then he is not satisfied and continues to force Balram to search for the coin. Balram himself becomes perplexed and, in the end, takes out a coin from his own pocket and gives to him who feels happy and satisfied.

Pinky Madam's insult hurts him and makes him alone because nobody is with him to take sides with him while Mr Mukesh's insult makes him think over the mean mentality of the rich man but at this time, Mr Ashok is on his side. Again also the difference of sex counts.

It is a part of human psychology that he sets his own parameters of success and defines it accordingly. But, the parameters, though individually a creation of his mind, are not his own; they are somewhere consciously or unconsciously governed by the things and persons whom he appreciates and loves to embrace. Balram Halwai has his ideal man in Vijay, the bus conductor, whom he follows consciously and unconsciously in life. Vijay, the pigherd's son has got success in life by availing of the opportunities to the maximum. People said that he "somehow befriended a politician" whom he let "his beak in his backside" (31). Balram wishes to be like Vijay and to be in possession of "a uniform, a pay cheque, a shiny whistle" (31) so that he may look important like him.

From a bus conductor, he switches over to politics. He becomes the supporter of the Great Socialist and delivers a speech in front of a tea shop in the village. Later he joins public service wearing "a white Nehru cap on his head" and "rings of solid gold on eight of his fingers" (103). Even in real life he becomes a follower of Vijay who makes the Stork bow down before him as a sign of respect. The presence of Vijay always remains imprinted in his mind. He learns driving and succeeds in becoming a chauffeur of the Stork family. It results in the khaki uniform that he longs for. The people living in the darkness know the value of the khaki uniform. His happiness knows no bound when he sees himself "reflected in the glass panes—all in khaki" (68) and now wishes for "a silver whistle" that will make him feel in paradise. Even his brother Kishan feels happy over his success in coming out of the mess because of "a uniform and a good master" (85). Later, the servant Balram in khaki uniform enters the Black Fort and becomes free from traditional values and embraces the immorality and dishonesty which make him spit at God. The man in khaki murders his master to make himself free from the stigma of a slave. What Balram does is achieved by Vijay. He is simply translating his ideal man into the real man in him. Like him, he does not mind to dip his beak into anything and at one place with his master becomes one body. Like him, he drinks and puts his beak into anything. The mother, father and Vijay somehow are fused in the personality of Balram Halwai who, later becomes the master with his master's wealth and name.

Munna is named as Balram by the teacher Krishna. First, the teacher thinks of the name Ram but there is already one boy whose name is Ram. Hence, he calls him 'Balram' and asks him whether he knows who Balram was. He tells him that "He was the sidekick of the god Krishna" (14) and asks him whether he knows his name. He tells him that his name is Krishna and so Balram will be the sidekick of the teacher Krishna. Somewhere in the corner of his mind, he keeps this name which makes him feel later in the novel that he is Krishna himself who has come here to guide his Arjuna. As he is named the white tiger by the inspector, a kind of superiority enters him. He thinks himself better than other students and, hence, also feels the same when he becomes a chauffeur to the Stork family. When he finds his master Mr Ashok weak and disappointed after the exit of Pinky Madam, he exhorts in the manner adopted by Krishna in the battlefield. He thinks that his master is Arjuna and he himself has the responsibility of being Krishna who has to instil courage and enthusiasm in life. He compares himself with Krishna who was also a chauffeur like him.

What will happen if the Kauravas are not destroyed? What will happen when the evil will embrace the whole world? Hence, the Kauravas were to be defeated for the welfare of the world. Krishna thinks of the world and the religion. Here, Balram as Krishna is selfish and thinks only of his welfare. What will happen if Mr Ashok does not live? What will happen if Mr Ashok returns to Dhanbad? "When the master's life is in chaos, so is the servant's. I thought, *Maybe he's sick of Delhi now. Will he go back to Dhanbad? What happens to me then?* My belly churned" (185). Arjuna is frustrated because of the relatives whom he has to kill. Here Mr Ashok is sick of life and, hence, drinks too much to forget his relationship with Pinky Madam with whom he married in spite of the opposition from his father. He does not find any point of living now but Balram as Krishna asks him to "believe in God, then good things will happen" (186). Actually he has fear not for Mr Ashok but for himself that what will happen if he dies. Who will pay him three and a half thousand rupees a month? The fear of the loss of money makes him look after Mr Ashok like a wife who makes sure of food, sleep and health. Hence, Krishna in Balram is selfish. It was the teacher in the village who got the upper hand and now he becomes Krishna and gets the upper hand over his master Mr Ashok.

What one sees and acts has a link with the consciousness that makes perception possible. Some perceptions are imprinted on the screen of consciousness while those which are repressed enter the domain of sub-consciousness which works in a dream. The dream of stiff toes always haunts him. This dream is connected with the memory of his mother whose toes remained unburnt because of the mud in the river Ganga. He does not like to watch Hindi movies, the reason being that the ideal is offered before the public while the reality is that it never happens in real life. Hindi movies make the culprit dream of the ghost "with bloody fingers, saying, Mur-der-er" which "does not happen like that in real life" (313). Somewhere, he feels the possibility of the dream and also the ghost of Mr Ashok. Hence, he does not like to go to watch Hindi movies. Once he dreams of Granny who comes on a water buffalo but after that she never comes in his dream. The real nightmare makes him sweat but he gets over it soon. After coming to Bangalore, he performs the last rites for the family members so that they may not come in his dream. He prays for all his aunts, cousins, nephews, nieces and even the water-buffalo. He states: "Who knows who has lived and who has not?" (314). He imagines the souls of his brother Kishan and granny Kusum and prays to let him live in peace. The story of the murder of 17 members of the family in a north Indian village makes him throw the newspaper in such disgust that he stops "reading the newspaper for a few months after that. Just to be safe" (314). He does not wish to live with the burden and, hence, dissociates himself completely from the family by performing the last rite. He is a white tiger who neither has a family nor friendship because it will not be safe for him from the point of view of his position of being the boss. He is a real entrepreneur who does not have the word 'sentiment' in his dictionary.

It is desire that motivates a man who tries his best to get it satisfied. Balram who longs for the golden hair searches for the strands of the golden hair of the beautiful girls and in the end becomes sick when he succeeds in having sex with them. Needless to say, the secret avenues of his unqualified longing about the golden hair that he speaks of are suppressed hungers. This longing is not the outcome of any random thought, rather its seeds can be seen in his boyhood that he passed in the village Laxmangarh. He shares the description of the village with the Chinese Premier and says:

> A stiff cardboard-backed poster for a pornographic film was tied to the back of his cycle—what traditional Indian village is complete without its blue-movie theatre, sir? A cinema across the river showed such films every night; two and a half hour fantasias with names like *He Was a True Man*, or *We Opened Her Diary*, or *The Uncle Did It*, featuring golden –haired women from American or lonely ladies from Hong Kong—or so I'm guessing, Mr Premier, since it's not like I ever joined the other young men and went to see one of these films! (23)

When he is a boy, he listens from others about the pornographic movies and the golden-haired women. Certainly he guesses what happens in the film on the basis of the information that he collects from others. He does not go to watch the movie—maybe because of the poverty or the strict control of granny. But, the title of the film like 'He was a True Man' makes him ponder over the characteristics of a true man. Hence, the seeds that are sown in the village through the mentioning of the pornographic film are nurtured properly when he comes to Delhi and later in Bangalore where they turn into trees that provide him the forbidden fruits that he eats with taste. Later, he becomes sick of the golden-haired women and declares that Indian women are the best on the basis of his experiences. Though in a few seconds, he thinks over it and switches over to Nepali women and rates Indian women as second best. His priority for the Nepali women has psychological reasons which result in making up his mind. As he transforms himself from servant to master, he removes the dress of a servant and wears what his master wore in order to become the master. Master Ashok loved a Nepali woman and this love awakens Balram who is the new avatar of master Ashok for the love. Hence, he changes his opinion on women and calls Nepali women best and Indian women second best.

Balram is not an ordinary man but a thinking man like his father. Basically there is a continuous struggle in his mind about whether he should become a man or remain a servant. When he opts to be a man, he thinks of the ways. The red bag becomes the source that will change his position. It is the devil that tempts him to take the bag. Initially he does not wish to be tempted and decides not "to look at the red bag" which seems to be a torture like Pinky Madam in her short skirts. When he looks at the rearview mirror, he finds a creature that seems to incite him to steal the bag convincing him that it is not stealing because it is not Mr Ashok's money but of the poor people like him. The creature in the mirror convinces Balram: "*See—Mr Ashok is giving money to all these politicians in Delhi so that they will excuse him from the tax he has to pay. And who owns that tax, in the end? Who but the ordinary people of this country—you*" (244)! The creature in the mirror is not any other creature but a reflection of his own personality. The same also happens when at a traffic signal, a driver spits and the spitting twice turns into two puddles which seem to be living things that speak to Balram. Again, the two puddles are the images of his imagination that concentrates on the red bag and the dilemma of whether to steal or not. The left puddle and the right puddle are the two contradictory voices of his conscience. The left puddle dissuades him from taking any action against Mr Ashok with the plea that his father wants him to be an honest man. Mr Ashok never hits him or spits on him; he gives a salary of rupees 4,000 that he raises from time to time without his asking and also reminds him of the threat that the Stork will follow the Buffalo in the treatment of his family if he runs away. But, the right puddle persuades him with more convincing reasons to take action against Mr Ashok. It asks him to be a man, the dream that his father saw, reminding him of the cruelty of the master who makes him responsible for the hit-and-run case. Regarding the salary, it says that what the master gives is not adequate in a city. It also provokes him over ways the point of Mr Ashok's threatening which can make any man's blood boil. The two puddles that come to life are the two images of his personality that clash because of the opposite opinions. Mr Ashok gives him a hundred-rupee note while earlier he takes out a one-thousand rupee note and asks Balram that he will take the responsibility of the expenditure of his marriage. Then, Balram becomes possessive and thinks that the master can do anything in his life. He speculates that these masters still own them and their "body, soul, and arse" (170). When he goes to defecate, he seems to see "a thin black fellow" who grins back at him. He goes near the fellow and smiles. The fellow's laughing makes all the crappers laugh. Mark the excerpt for the echo of laughing and the warning therein:

> He began to laugh—and I began to laugh—and then all the crappers laughed together.
>
> 'We'll take care of your wedding expenses,' I shouted.

> 'We'll take care of your wedding expenses! he shouted back.
>
> 'We'll even fuck your wife for you, Balram!'
>
> 'We'll even fuck your wife for you, Balram!'
>
> He began laughing –laughing so violently that he fell down face-first into the ground, still laughing, exposing his stained arse to the stained sky of Delhi. (261)

This imaginary scene and the reality associated with it convince him that the master can fuck his wife in the name of doing favour to Balram. Hence, he becomes conscious of the injustice and exploitation done to the poor. Then he makes up his mind to kill his master and steal the red bag full of money.

In Bangalore, Balram finds the boom in outsourcing and plans to be associated with it. But, the idea of outsourcing is not the outcome of his mind; it still has its seeds in Mr Ashok whose cloak he has now worn. When Uma finds Mr Ashok upset, he shares with her that he wants to do "something else. Something clean. Like outsourcing" (210). When he observes outsourcing in Bangalore, he plans to be in it in any way. He also finds a gateway through outsourcing that will lead him to the place where "real estate, wealth, power, sex" flow. Now, he is not Balram Halwai, he is "Ashok Sharma, North Indian entrepreneur settled in Bangalore" (302). He has written the new word "entrepreneur" on the slate of his destiny erasing the earlier written words "a sweet-maker". He hires a Toyota Qualis, earns money and soon becomes the master of many Qualis vehicles. "Once I was a driver to a master, but now I am a master of drivers" (302).

Balram believes in the Darwinian law of the survival of the fittest. It is quite natural that the weak will be wiped out by the strong. From the very beginning he knows that Mr Ashok is weak, a lamb in the real sense, and so thinks of sacrificing the Lamb for his gains. He wishes to cut the Mongoose's throat but he is strong. Mr Ashok is the right ladder by which he climbs and achieves his target. Mr Ashok shares with Balram that his "way of living is all wrong" and he has no "courage to change it" because he does not have "the balls" (237). He has failed to translate what he wished in his life. It is his cowardice that he let other people exploit him. When Balram comes to know these facts of Mr Ashok's life, he feels pity but along with it he thinks of growing rich for which he has to sacrifice this Lamb. He eats the lamb to become the white tiger.

The white tiger has neither friends nor sentiments. He is tagged as "working class hero" (264) but none, except the Chinese Premier knows that this hero is "not a brave man" (275). This hero, rather anti-hero who was not considered superior to Cuddles and Puddles, advocates the philosophy that "Let animals live like animals; let humans live like humans" (276) so that people may get their due place in the society. The ways he adopts are wrong and lead a man nowhere. But, the tiger that cannot be caged breaks "the law of his land" in order to "turn bad news into good news" (38). This tiger that crushed the brain of Mr Ashok through the Johnnie Walker Black bottle cares for his own brain and, so, does not use a mobile phone and the things that "corrode a man's brains, shrink his balls, and dry up his semen" (38). If the brain is lost, what will remain with him? If his balls shrink and the semen dries up, how will he enjoy sex? A body with brains makes a master while a body without brains gives birth to slavery. He is not born to be a slave, he imagines with his mind that makes him see the beautiful in the world.

The volcano in Balram has erupted and the Freudian lava has spread making the land fertile. The white tiger is now at peace because of the mind that now sees neither dreams nor hallucinations arising out of conflicts. The tiger Ashok goes ahead forwarding his technology and does not look behind to the place where he ate the Lamb Mr Ashok and sacrificed the lives of all his family members. He has done his duty by performing the last rites for the family members and paid tribute to Mr Ashok by adopting his name in the world of outsourcing, the field where the Lamb wished to graze. The nightmares are over but the dreams of utopia refresh his mind. He dreams of starting a school where poor children in

Bangalore will be taught the facts that will make them white tigers. Such a school will not corrupt "anyone's head with prayers and stories about Gandhi" (320). With these white tigers, he will become the boss who will put the assistant commissioner of police "on a cycle and have Asif knock him over it with the Qualis" (320). This is the dreaming that he does now and he knows well that it will "turn out to be nothing" (320).

WORK CITED

Adiga, Aravind. *The White Tiger*. New Delhi: HarperCollins, 2008. **Print.**

11

Beak into Anything: The Forbidden Landscape

> Now, it had been a long time since I had dipped my beak into anything, sir, and the pressure had built up. The girl would be so young—seventeen or eighteen—and you know what girls taste like at that age, like watermelons. Any diseases, of body or mind, get cured when you penetrate a virgin. These are known facts. (192-93)

Sex is a means that unlocks the gate of love and shows the heavenly pleasure. Indian culture gives priority to love—true love over sex—but never neglects its importance in uniting the thread of marital relationship. But, when, sex becomes an end and love is simply used as a means to acquire the end, it degrades the name and depth of love. It is tragic that in the era of globalisation everything has become a commodity. This consumer culture has turned sex into a commodity and has set the price. Everything is for sale, how can sex be away from this view? The Western culture has injected the poison of consumerism in India where now people feel it honourable to set the value for sex. Buy or steal. This is the way of life that has been embraced. Give the girl her price and enjoy her body. If not, steal either by force or by love. Love is the weapon that is used to entrap the innocent girl who later comes to know the trap of the body but by then it is too late. Now, because of the freedom from both sides, a new trend in the form of lesbianism or homosexuality is in the air. Success is the priority even at the cost of the body. Aravind Adiga's *The White Tiger* is full of such forbidden landscapes that are dotted with homosexuality and prostitution.

Adiga's protagonist Balram Halwai is the white tiger not in name but in the real sense. This tiger who loves "kebabs of chicken, mutton, and beef" runs in the jungle of five-star hotels to enjoy "sluts of all nationalities" (200). Whenever this tiger, does not dip his "beak into anything" he feels restless because of retaining "semen" that leads to "evil movements in the fluids" (250) of the upper body. This tiger strongly believes in the treatment of diseases through sex-therapy. He recommends the penetration into a virgin of seventeen or eighteen years old if one wants to be cured of any disease. What a treatment! This tiger should start a clinic and provide girls for curing diseases. There is no benefit in being the master of drivers or the director of a school. The White Tiger Clinic: Miracles through Sex will give him pleasures of social service and also will help him in making a messiah who brings peace after removing the diseases of the body and the mind.

The tiger Balram Halwai in Bangalore goes to five-star hotels to "buy girls" because he thinks that "it's not right to buy and sell women who live in bird cages and get treated like animals" (304). But, in Delhi, he did not do so. He was interested in golden-hair women and in homosexuality. There are instances that prove that he is a homosexual. His ideal icon is Vijay who became a bus-conductor and got a uniform not because of his intelligence but because of his ability in befriending a politician whom he let his beak dip in his backside. Vijay did what he could do to be a successful man. He was "the first entrepreneur" whom he knew.

Balram Halwai gets his man in Mr Ashok Sharma whom he serves with love. It is his love for his master that he becomes "sentimental" to the extent that he needs "some paper napkins" (46). When Mr Ashok and Pinky Madam come to Laxmangarh, he asks the caretaker: "I love Mr Ashok so much you must let me serve him lunch" (82). The cook agrees and Balram Halwai serves his beloved master. Even now, when Mr Ashok is no more, he recalls him in his mind's eye. Mark the two excerpts for the descriptions that reflect his leaning towards his master:

> Mr Ashok's face reappears now in my mind's eye as it used to every day when I was in his service—reflected in my rearview mirror. It was such a handsome face that sometimes I couldn't take my eyes off it. Picture a six-foot-tall fellow, broad-shouldered, with a landlord's powerful, punishing forearms; yet always gentle (*almost* always—except for that time he punched Pinky Madam in the face) and kind to those around him, even his servants and driver. (46)
>
> ...
>
> The car came to a stop. Our bodies crossed each other again, our scents were exchanged once more, and I was again the driver and servant, and Mr Ashok was again the passenger and master. (112)

This description of the master's body tells a different story. He cares for his master even when Pinky Madam goes away. Like a wife he cares for him. He is a servant and being a servant he knows "his master's intestinal tract from end to end—from lips to anus" (141). When he signs the affidavit and takes the responsibility of Pinky Madam's crime, he imagines that he will go to jail. What happens in the jail? How will he save himself from "the big hairy, dirty men"? He remembers a story in the *Murder Weekly* about a man who pretends to have AIDS to escape from buggery in the jail. But, is there any guarantee that they will leave him? It is also possible that they may regard him as "a professional bugger" and bugger him even more. He has not yet gone to the jail but thinks of buggery and the things related with homosexuality. He also mentions an occasion that makes Mr Ashok and Balram one body. Mark the excerpt for the homosexual aroma:

> I swore not to look in the rearview mirror again that night. Now I understood why the city looked so different—why my beak was getting stiff as I was driving.
>
> Because he was horny. And inside that sealed car, master and driver had somehow become one body that night.
>
> It was with great relief that I drove the Honda into the gate of the Maurya Sheraton Hotel, and brought that excruciating trip to an end. (199)

The driver becomes the master and the master the driver. Who is the victim and who is the victimiser? The important thing is the forbidden fruit tasted by both satisfactorily. The victim victimises the victimiser and the victimiser victimises the victim. And the story goes on.

When Balram Halwai goes to the National Zoo with Dharam, he takes permission from Mr Ashok who allows him to go, and feels happy. Then, he sees a small dark man belonging to a servant class. Mr Ashok talks with him and the small man shows his respect and goes away. "They looked like two men who had just concluded a deal" (274). Balram is talking of a deal but what this deal is, is secret which lies in homosexuality. When he murders his master and runs away, he does not forget to take Dharam with him because he knows that the police will arrest him as an accomplice and then the wild men will bugger him. He thinks: "If I left him there now, the police would certainly arrest him as an accomplice. They would throw him into jail with a bunch of wild men—and you know what happens to little boys when they get put into dens like that, sir" (287). He talks of buggery but blames the President of America who "has made buggery perfectly legal in his country" (305). The forbidden fruit is made available for all. "Men are marrying other men instead of women", the result of which is "the decline of the white man" (305). He does not use the mobile phone which was invented by the Japanese to "diminish the white man's brain and balls" (305).

Now, from homosexuality, he switches over to the fair sex—Pinky Madam whose low black dress makes his 'beak' big. He suffers from a moral dilemma and does not know what to do because he cannot think of sex with her. She is the wife of his master and the wife of the master is mother-like. How can he think of sex with his mother? Hence, he hates her for "wearing that dress" but hates his "beak even more for what it was doing" (143). He presents his moral dilemma thus:

> When she sat in the back, I could see half her boobs hanging out of her clothes each time had to look in the rearview mirror.

> This put me in a very bad situation, sir. For one thing, my beak was aroused, which is natural in a healthy young man like me. On the other hand, as you know, master and mistress are like father and mother to you, so how can you get excited by the mistress?
>
> I simply avoided looked at the rearview mirror. If there was a crash, it wouldn't be my fault. (143)

When she comes and asks for him to make the special traditional type of tea, he feels relief not because of the order but "at least her boobs were covered" (145). Both the master and mistress in their intoxicated condition behave "like animals", the master "pushing his hand up and down her thigh" (159) which has the mistress "giggling", without being aware that they are in car with the driver Balram who sees them in the rearview mirror. In the room, he also hears sounds of sex enjoyment by Mr Ashok and Pinky Madam. It is sex which makes a man and a woman shriek to release the fluid of the life-force that gives immense pleasure. Mark the excerpt for the sex between Mr Ashok and Pinky Madam:

> The two of them had gone into their bedroom. I heard shouting from inside. On tiptoe, I went to the closed door. I put my ear to the wood.
>
> Shouting rose from both sides—followed by a scream—followed by the sound of man's flesh slapping woman's flesh. (155)

Later Balram sees "debauchery inside the car" which he never approves. But, he is a driver and being a driver he remains silent. He cannot stop his master who is busy in celebrating "the carnival of fun" (203). When Mr Ashok is on the way back, he begins "the petting and kissing" with a Nepali girl. He wonders: "My God, and he a man who was still lawfully married to another woman (209)! The Nepali girl is his old lover Uma. She is not a Nepali but looks like a Nepali because of her eyes. When Mr Ashok asks her to go home with the driver, she refuses because of the mentality of the drivers who think that "any unmarried woman they see is a whore" (211). She does not trust any Delhi drivers who sell "drugs, and prostitutes and

God knows what else" (211). This master becomes a debauchee running after sex and does not feel hesitation in having sex with the whore. He enjoys sex with a Ukrainian student without having inner satisfaction.

Balaram Halwai who is "a surprise package" is taken by the old driver to the red-light district where he is stunned to see "the gorgeous women" who jeer and taunt at him "from behind their grilled windows" begging him "to dip beak into them" (58). What he sees is not the women but commodities for sale. He is shocked to see the commodification of bodies. Women, the wares are for sale.

Every type of woman is available. Even eunuchs and small boys are also turned into commodities meant for sex. Later, he observes the culture of Delhi, the roads of which are full of many painted women with whom men, in the midst of the traffic, seem "to negotiate a price" (198) with them. The driver with the pink lips tells him that his master likes film actreses whom he takes to the hotel where he "hammers" them. At the red light, Mr Ashok and Balram see a girl with large boobs which seem to be like brinjals. Mark the description of her chest:

> I had stopped the car at a traffic signal; a girl began crossing the road in a tight T-shirt, her chest bobbling up and down like three kilogrammes of brinjals in a bag. I glanced at the rearview mirror—and there was Mr Ashok, his eyes also bobbing up and down. (199)

Is there any secret that the white tiger sees the breasts of women? He sees a poor woman with full breasts lying on the floor. Though she is poor, she is carefree. Mark the excerpt:

> Not far from me I saw a woman lying on the floor, with nice full breasts inside a tight blouse. She was snoring. I could see a one-rupee note stuffed into her cleavage, its lettering and colour visible through the weave of her bright green blouse. She had no luggage. That was all she had in the world. One rupee. And yet look at her—snoring blissfully, without a care in the world.
>
> Why couldn't things be so simple for me? (249)

The white tiger cares for his brain but this brain remains polluted because of sex. Sex is present in his mind. Even when he goes to the road where books are being sold, he sees the books in foreign language. He is confident that the books give "a kind of electricity buzzing" and erect the brain like a man who gets erect when he sees "girls wearing tight jeans" (206).

Balram Halwai is a driver and being a driver it is his mentality to use abusive words. Drivers abuse one another. When the masters are in the malls for shopping, the drivers wait in the parking place where they chew *paan*, gossip and release ammonia. Balram goes to "a clump of trees" where he takes "an ammonia break". Mark the two lines for releasing ammonia before and after:

> Our piss hit the bark of the tree just inches apart. (202)
>
> I zipped up and ran, wiping my wet fingers on the back of my trousers. (203)

On the forbidden landscape, there are some dirty spots which in spite of being dirty become beauty marks that help in getting the beak bigger. *What a fucking joke* (7), divine arses (8), sister-fucker (34), Fuck off (60), Nepali fucker (60), a fucking genius (160), *fucking* traffic jam (240), *totally* fucked (270), this fucking business (292) etc. are some abusive words which are freely used in the novel without caring for the evil influence that they will have. But, he knows only one mantra—how to make the 'beak' big. He succeeds in his mission through abusive words and sexual expressions. Here are some instances of sexual expressions that have come from Balram's brain:

> Kishan got two weeks to dip his beak into his wife, and then he was packed off to Dhanbad. (51)
>
> I wondered what was going on with her—was she having a fight with her husband? Was he not sticking it to her well in bed? (72)
>
> The moment the Mongoose left, I swear, the skirts became even shorter. (143)

> When she sat in the back, I could see half her boobs hanging out of her clothes each time had to look in the rearview mirror. (143)

> I walked with the old driver, my mouth open, gaping at all the gorgeous women jeering and taunting me from behind their grilled windows—all of them begging me to dip my beak into them! (58)

Abusive phrases like "immense pyramids of shit" (255), "fuck your wife for you" (261) and "stained arse to the stained sky of Delhi" (261) etc. add the glamour to the forbidden landscape. When he dishes out Indian sex with the Western spices, he offers "*paan*" and "hot milk" so that the Western reader's brain may get erected again and again. Do Indians think of beak, arse, boobs, women's begging for dipping beak? Or Is it Adiga's brain that gets erected and begins to work? The beak is in the brain. This is his beak that makes him see arses of 36, 000, 004 gods. When will the white tiger kiss gods' feet in place of arses? He has his readymade suggestion for curing any disease whether of body or mind through dipping the 'beak' into a virgin. His sex market has earned a high profit. He has changed the previous script of developing the body of culture into a culture of the body. Thanks to the boom of consumerism that has turned the world into post-modernism where everything is for sale. One day, when the tiger becomes old, he will be forced to think because of his approaching death that the 'beak' is only a means of releasing lust that turns a man into an animal. What counts is man. Certainly, in old age, the 'beak' of the white tiger will become weak to the extent that it will not be able to colour the forbidden landscape. Then, "the beak into anything" will become "the beak into nothing" and out of this nothing, he will take out something which will give him meaning to his life.

Work Cited

Adiga, Aravind. *The White Tiger*. New Delhi: HarperCollins, 2008. **Print**.

12

Topography: Spatial Identity

Space, time and environment are the ingredients that determine the authenticity of a narrative, be it a novel or a drama or any form of literature. The narrative becomes dull and meaningless until or unless it speaks of its space and time. To compare a piece of literature of a particular country to another is not proper because of the difference in culture and values. What is considered a part of culture in a country may be inhibition in another country. To judge literature on the basis of a country leads nowhere. Every country has its own culture which may differ from another country and the particular values and traditions make its identity.

Every literary artist portrays the landscape to show its distinctiveness though there are some universal characteristics that are found in every country. A reader is inquisitive by nature and this nature forces him to know about time and space. He knows that he cannot compare any culture with his own culture. When one studies American literature, an Indian reader cannot go into the depth if he judges it with the parameters of Indian literature. To enjoy literature of any particular country, one needs to have the knowledge of the country and its culture, otherwise it will be a biased study. Aravind Adiga in his novel *The White Tiger* has employed the technique of space and time. He makes a tour of the country where he shows the river and lands, mountains, cities and villages. He presents the contemporary picture of the Post-Independence India and attempts to show that in spite of the claim of having realised the concept of shining India, some of its landscapes remain in darkness.

For Adiga, it is the river Ganga that divides India into two—India of Light and India of Darkness. The places that are near the ocean belong to the India of Light. The contesting terms for two Indias—India and Bharat—representing the land where the city people live and the land where the village people live respectively are not new. Adiga has depicted these two Indias that differ in attitude and values. The protagonist Balram Halwai in *The White Tiger* is settled in Bangalore, the India of Light as a North Indian entrepreneur though he came from Laxmangarh, the land that belongs to the India of Darkness. He begins with Laxmangarh, goes to Dhanbad, shifts to Delhi and finally settles in Bangalore. No doubt, Adiga has attempted to give a picture of the contemporary India but to consider it as the final picture will be an injustice to India as a whole. This is India from the specs of a driver who pulls his roots from the native land and grows them in the city vase.

Balram Halwai shares with the Chinese Premier about the divisions of India into two Indias on the basis of the ocean and the river. It is the river that brings darkness to India.

What he says is not true. It is the river Ganga which has given birth to Ganga-Yamuna culture. If the rivers had not been there, not only India but the whole world also would have been a barren land. He talks of Bodh Gaya, a popular town because of Lord Buddha who "sat under a tree and found his enlightenment and started Buddhism which then spread to the whole world, including China" (48). This place is a few miles away from his native land Laxmangarh. He wonders that Laxmangah is in darkness in spite of Lord Buddha and so guesses that he would not have walked here. Rather he might have run to go to the other side without looking behind. A small branch of the river Ganga flows outside Laxmangarh. The boats sail in the river and bring the things related to daily life on Monday. He depicts the street which splits into two because of a strip of sewage. In shops on either side are sold the daily-use things like adulterated rice, cooking oil, kerosene, biscuits, cigarettes etc. These shops create the scene of a market that ends at the place where the temple devoted to Lord Hanuman is situated. Hanuman is an ideal of "absolute fidelity, love and devotion" (19). But, Balram is wrong when he says that Hanuman is "everyone's favourite god in the Darkness" (19) while the truth is that he is worshipped by all without considering the hierarchy which is the creation of his mind.

Ironically, he calls Laxmangarh a "typical Indian village paradise" because of the facilities. But these ideal facilities are in the pages of the file while the reality is that it is hell where electricity poles are no longer in use. Water taps are broken while children are "too lean and short for their age and with over-sized heads from which vivid eyes shine, like the guilty conscience of the government of India" (20). Families of pigs can be found through sewage. He tells the Chinese Premier that he will find the water buffalo at the door of his house. The water buffalo is given more importance than an individual because of the milk that she gives. Feeding fresh grass to her becomes an important task of the women so that she may become fat. Her fatness determines her capacity of giving milk. Milk is the commodity that is sold in the market. As she is the earning member because of her milk, she sits all the day "in her own stupendous crap" and becomes "the dictator" (20) of the house.

Women in the house prepare meal for the buffalo and perform the daily domestic activities right from winnowing rice to fighting. He states:

> Once you walk into the house, you will see—if any of them are still living, after what I did—the women. Working in the courtyard. My aunts and cousins and Kusum, my granny. One of them preparing the meal for the buffalo; one winnowing rice; one squatting down, looking through the scalp of another woman, squeezing the ticks to death between her fingers. Every now and then they stop their work, because it is time to fight. This means throwing metal vessels at one another, or pulling each other's hair, and then making up, by putting kisses on their palms and pressing them to the others' cheeks. At night they sleep tighter, their legs falling one over the other, like one creature, a millipede. (21)

The fighting and quarrelling are not forever as they soon make up and love. These are the innocent activities and pleasures which are far away from the cunningness and trickery of the city life. Gray's line: "Far from the madding crowd" suits the life of the simple villagers. Women sleep in one corner while men and boys in another. As soon as it is morning, life begins. Balram with his father unties the water buffalo and takes her to the pond for her bath. What Balram depicts is partially true because nowadays villages are not so as depicted because people have become conscious of the change. Now, villages are provided the basic facilities of infrastructure and means of communications.

Balram now talks of the school which is "a paradise within a paradise" (32). The school teacher who has not got his salary for the last six months steals the lunch money provided by the government for giving three *rotis*, yellow *daal* and pickles. He is a low salary paid teacher but the charm of the government job is the numerous incidental advantages. The school uniforms meant for the school boys are sold in the neighbouring village. No one holds the teacher responsible for this because one cannot "expect a man in a dung heap to smell sweet" (33). A school teacher is forced to indulge in corruption because of the salary which he does not get in time. Corruption is present everywhere and no one can deny this fact which Adiga has mentioned here through Balaram Halwai. In almost all the small villages the tea shop becomes the focal point where people meet and come to know various things. In Laxmangarh, the tea shop is "the central point" where the bus from Gaya stops and the policemen park their jeep and go to the village "to bugger someone". In the evening, a man with "a stiff cardboard-backed poster for a pornographic film" tied to the cycle goes on his rounds to attract more people for the show. It is surprising why Adiga thinks of equipping the village cinema hall with pornographic films. For him, a village is incomplete "without its blue-movie theatre" (23). This is not true. Advertisements of pornographic film in a village are unthinkable. Where has Adiga seen such an advertisement?

How will the people in Laxmangarh manage to watch the blue movies when most of them are unemployed? Thousands of people in the villages who are unemployed have lost any hope of getting a job. Balram works at the tea shop but he overhears the conversations at every table in order to learn something or the other. The tea shop becomes the centre of attraction particularly when election is round the corner. The tea shop owner has already sold the "fingerprints" of every boy working at the shop. Voting in the election is a mockery because booths are captured. The Great Socialist who indulges in corruption and murder is the boss of the darkness. This time the landlords are also contesting elections and, hence, it will be a close one. But, finally, the Great Socialist wins by virtue of his muscle power. The children of the four landlords—the Stork, the Raven, the Wild Boar and the Buffalo who exploit the villagers—now live in Dhanbad or in Calcutta because of the fear of Naxals. These landlords exploit the villagers because of their power and money. Land, roads, river, grassy fields etc. belong to them and, hence, one who wishes to use them will have to pay. The Great Socialist and the landlords shake hands and become the protectors of the villagers whom they exploit.

It is the Black Fort that attracts Balram but his granny makes him afraid of the lizard that lives in it. When he succeeds in getting a job in the Stork family, he feels happy because the dream of having the uniform has come true. He comes to Laxmangarh with Mr Ashok and Pinky Madam and attempts to enter the Black Fort. He crosses the pond and enters it from where he sees his village which seems to be "the most beautiful sight on earth" (42) but develops a kind of superiority which makes him hate the traditional values and culture of the village, and so while leaning out from the edge of the fort, he starts spitting again and again. His spiting is the spitting at the village culture. From innocence he enters the zone of experiences which fill ambition in him to the extent that he wishes to be the master. He sees what is beautiful in the world. He is born not to be a slave but a master.

Now, the journey that begins from Laxmangarh finds its first milestone in Delhi via Dhanbad.

Delhi, for Adiga's Balram, is not the capital of one India but of two Indias because of the people from the Light and the Darkness who reside here. Old Delhi and Gurgaon are the two areas belonging to the traditional and modern people respectively. Mr Ashok, the master of Balram, lives in Gurgaon, which is a mini America. The Old Delhi is "full of things that modern world forgot all about—rickshawas, old stone buildings, and Muslims" (251). Delhi is a place where one will be lost. When Balram comes here for the first time, he does not find his way because of the confusion regarding the roads that "look the same, all of them go around and around grassy circles in which men are sleeping or eating or playing cards, and then four roads shoot off from that grassy circle, and then you go down one road, and you hit another grassy circle where men are sleeping or playing cards, and then four more roads go off from it" (119). People who come from the darkness reside on the sides of the road as they do not have houses to live in. They can be recognised by "their thin bodies, by the animal-like way they live under the huge bridges and overpass, making fires and washing and taking lice out of their hair while the cars roar past them" (120). They leave the villages in order to have the light in their life but unfortunately they have to live in the darkness which becomes a part of their fate. It seems odd that they build homes for the rich but remain homeless and fail to have the minimum needs necessary for living. For the drivers, they pose problems as they "never wait for a red light—simply dashing across the road on impulse" (120).

Delhi, if seen from a driver's point of view, is "a crazy city" (118) where "civilisation can appear and disappear within five minute" (281). It is Delhi that can make a master courteous to the extent that he likes to inform the driver about the time of return. Balram interrogates about the design and the naming of the roads. He guesses that the man who planned Delhi would be busy in celebration and drinking English wine resulting in naming the roads "that no one could remember" (120), otherwise he would have never made "F Block come after A Block and House Number 69 come after House Number 12" (120). Every road is named and neither servants nor masters know the name. Greater Kailash is the housing colony where "people of quality live" (217). But, the number system as well as the lettering system in the colonies follows no rule. In Delhi, apartment blocks with English names are in fashion. Buckingham Towers B Block is one of the best with a nice lobby equipped with lift. Delhi is well furnished with good roads but lack good people. Mark the excerpt about the general idea of Delhi and its people:

> The main thing to know about Delhi is that the roads are good, and the people are bad. The police are totally rotten. If they see you without a seat belt, you'll have to bribe them a hundred rupees. Our masters are not such a great lot, either. When they go for their late-night parties, it's hell for us. You sleep in the car, and the mosquitoes eat you alive. (124)

Traffic and pollution are the integral part of Delhi where vehicles can be seen pushing "for space on the road". In Delhi, there is only one Ring Road while Beijing has a dozen. The result is traffic jams. Balram is not sure whether Indians will ever "catch up with the Chinese" when in Delhi "nothing is planned" (138). Pollution in Delhi force the people on the vehicles to "have a handkerchief wrapped around their faces" (133). The red light gives a view of "a row of men with black glasses and masks on their faces, as if the whole city were out on a bank heist that morning" (133). It is quite natural for the people of Delhi to wear the masks, otherwise "the air is so bad in Delhi that it takes then years off a man's life" (133).

Balram also differentiates Delhi on the basis of the cars, the dark eggs running on the roads. People with eggs need not breathe the outside air because of the clean air-conditioned air that they have inside it. Sometimes, the egg cracks and shows the gold-bangle hand of a woman who throws out a mineral water bottle and then the window is closed and "the egg is resealed" (134). The poor people are also responsible in increasing the pollution level. When it is winter, not to talk of electrical heaters or gas heaters or logs of wood in fireplaces like the rich people they do not have houses to live in. The homeless burn something to keep them warm. They use cellophane which, when burnt, releases a white smoke that not only pollutes the atmosphere but makes one's stomach churn.

The post-Independence culture has brought the mall culture that knows only one language—the language of materialism. Money can give all the pleasures that a man needs. Everything is put in the scale of consumerism. There is nothing which is not for sale. This culture has created a distance from one heart to another heart. The material bond has swallowed the emotional bond to the full. A human being, if poor, is not treated like a human being. What makes a man a human being is not the emotional relationship but the material one. The poor cannot think of entering the mall. Gurgaon, the modern Delhi, has shopping malls, each having a cinema hall on the main road. Rich people enjoy life by virtue of their money. Balram mentions PVR Saket, the scene of "a big cinema, which shows ten or twelve films at the same time, and charges over a hundred and fifty rupees per film" but the thing that makes it a particular place is the facilities of providing the places "to drink beer, dance, pick up girls" to make the rich people feel "a small bit of America in India" (204). Delhi which is a city of pomp and show is full of "grand hotels" like "the Sheraton, the Imperial, the Taj Palace, Taj Mansingh, the Oberoi, the Intercontinental, and many more" (200). These hotels are used for wine and sex. Beautiful girls—Indians and foreigners—are supplied to the rich people who enjoy sex with them. Though the mall culture with big grand hotels no doubt reflects the modernity, it sucks the values and traditions leaving men insolvent morally. The glamour of the modern culture makes the sheen of Indian values and traditions weak and tempts the people to eat the forbidden fruits which make him a part of the consumer culture that believes in price value for everything.

Balram thinks that Mr Ashok has taken the right decision of residing in Gurgaon which will make Pinky Madam comfortable and give her the feel of America. Though initially it was a place with "just water buffaloes and fat Punjabi farmer", it is now "the modernest suburb of Delhi" (122) with the office of big companies like American Express, Microsoft etc. The construction work in Gurgaon continues at night. Balram depicts the construction work thus: "big lights shine down from towers, and dust rises from pits, scaffolding is being erected, and men and animals, both shaken from their sleep and bleary and insomniac, go around and around carrying concrete rubble or bricks" (192). Amidst this modernity, he also mentions a roadside temple where he goes and puts a rupee "before the two resident pairs of divine arses" (187) and prays for the union and happy life for his master Mr Ashok and mistress Pinky Madam.

Balram never forgets to listen to the roads of Delhi with which he shows his affinity. He listens to Delhi and asks it to let him know of the civil war. He listens to its answer in positive and further enquires of "blood on the streets" (221). Roads are not roads for him but the human beings with whom he shares. The road knows his secret beforehand when he determines to murder his master. Every driver in Delhi is supposed to read the magazine, titled *Murder Weekly*, the price of which is only four rupees and fifty paisa. Though it narrates the stories of murder, rape and revenge, it never incites them to murder because of the end that makes them fear of consequence. Hence, in spite of fantasizing about the murder of the bosses, the driver does not gather courage to murder. That's why the Government of India "publishes" it and "sells" it just for four rupees and fifty paisa "so that even the poor can buy it" (125). Servants who are in the habit of quarrelling with one another do not hesitate in abusing. It is in their blood but they do it just for fun and amusement. The uniform, which makes Balram proud of himself, is not liked in Delhi where a driver in uniform looks like "monkey".

Delhi jails are full of drivers not because of the crime they have committed but because of the crime of their masters which they have taken on them. This is again the abuse of the capital that purchases a poor man in the name of faithfulness and devotion. Drivers go to jail loyally for their master. Balram himself becomes the victim and signs the affidavit declaring that he himself is responsible for the hit-and-run case. He is ready to go to jail for the crime of Pinky Madam. Delhi is also famous for medical facilities. Even the hospital has taken the place of five-star hotels where the rich people are treated well. Max is "one of Delhi's most famous private hospitals" which has a lobby that looks "as clean as the inside of a five-star hotel" (181). Delhi is incomplete without books which are for sale on Sunday on the footpaths. Shops are closed on this day while the restaurants release "the smell of fired food" that gets mixed with "the smell of rotting paper" (252).

Delhi and corruption are wedded to each other. Bribery is the thread that binds Delhi and corruption. When Mr Mukesh tells Mr Ashok that they have to grease "a couple of bureaucrats", he expresses his anger thus: "It seems like this is all I get to do in Delhi. Take money out of banks and bribe people. Is this what I came back to India for" (240)? After bribing a minister, they pass "the famous bronze statue of Gandhi leading his followers from darkness to the light" (281). Mr Mukesh asks him to reserve his judgment because "things are complicated in India" (137). Mr Ashok holds the political system responsible for the corruption. This corruption has its presence even in embassies. Mark the excerpt for the depiction of corruption:

> Foreign wine is very expensive in Delhi, because it's taxed. But the embassies get it in for free. They're supposed to drink their wine, but they sell it on the black market. I can get him other stuff too. Does he want golf balls? I've got people in the US Consulate who will sell me that. Does he want women? I can get that too. If he's into boys, no problem.' (127)

Foreigners come to India to know her culture and the way of enlightenment. Balram wonders why they go to the Himalayas, or to Benaras, or to Bodh Gaya. They go to these places in order to be enlightened. To think that getting into "weird poses of yoga", smoking hashish and shagging a *sadhu* can make them enlightened is an illusion. He asks them to "forget the Ganga—forget the ashrams" (275) and advises them to go straight to the National Zoo where they can have the real enlightenment.

To give a feel of the live picture, Adiga has mentioned names like "The House of Parliament, the Jantar Mantar, The Qutub, Raisina Hill (135), South Extension, Part Two—one of the best shopping areas in Delhi (232), Sahara Mall (198),

Connaught Place (156), Darya Ganja (252), Lodi Gardens (267), Jangpura (217), The Congress Party headquarter (133), Sonia Gandhi (134), bronze statues of Gandhi and Nehru (141)". The reader is conscious that he is in Delhi. What one thing that Adiga has done to make the description more real is the FIR. The number of the FIR, the address of website, the address and the phone numbers give the touch of the real happening in Delhi. The FIR and the wanted advertisement run thus:

> The missing man was employed as a driver of a Honda City vehicle at the time of the alleged incident. In this regard a case, FIR No. 438 / 05. P. S. Dhaula Kuan, Delhi, has been registered. He is also believed to be in possession of a bag filled with a certain quantity of cash. (32)
>
> ...any person having any information or clue about this missing man may kindly inform at CBI Web site (http://cbi.nic.in) e-mail ID (diccbi@cbi.nic.in), Fax No. 011-23011334. T No. 011-23014046 (Direct) 011-23015229 and 23015218 Extn. 210 and to the undersigned at the following address or telephone number or numbers given below.
>
> DP 3687 / 05
>
> SHO—Dhaula Kuan, New Delhi
>
> Tel: 28653200. 27641000 (39)

Adiga has attempted his best to depict Delhi as it is but even then the description is not wholly authentic. It is partly from the eyes of a driver who is in the habit of observing the things in flashes. Every girl on the road is not for sale. But, to Balram, every girl seems to bargain price for herself. Even Ms Uma, the beloved of Mr Ashok, does not wish to go home with the driver Balram because of the mean mentality of drivers. No doubt, the description sounds good and Adiga has done his best to intimate to the readers with every road to create the real Delhi but even then it is partially correct. Everybody is not corrupt. Still there are people who live a moral life and for whom everything is not for sale. He has presented either the higher class of Mr Ashok or the people of the lower class living on the roads and slums but he forgets a great sect of the middle and lower middle class. It is so because Balram has seen either the life of Laxmangarh where poverty rules or the life of the Stork family where the living standard is too high to imagine. It is the Stork who sends his son Mr Ashok to America. But, the middle class or lower middle class cannot afford that so easily. Hence, the image of Delhi at the micro level and of India at the macro level is not wholly authentic.

Words and names are the same but they interchange their places. The miracle, the seed of which sprouts in Delhi, comes to full bloom in Bangalore. Balram, after murdering his master and stealing the red bag full of money, comes to Bangalore, the second milestone in his life. Delhi designs and executes the plan for Balram; Bangalore that provides the climate of the flowering of the fruits brings it to life. The word 'slave' from Laxmangarh's dictionary changes into 'master' in Delhi's dictionary but it is Bangalore's authentic dictionary that finalises 'boss' as the right word. The Bangalore dictionary also changes the word from "Balram" to "Ashok Sharma". "A driver to a master" transforms into "a master of drivers". This is the milestone achieved by the white tiger Balram Halwai who treats his employees in a professional manner to the extent that when they complete their work, he kicks "them out of the office: no chitchat, no cup of coffee" because "a White Tiger keeps no friends" (302).

The thing that makes Balram different is his habit of friendship with the roots in the form of roads and streets. He tries to hear "Bangalore's voice" (297) after calming his nerves. He comes here and finds new people and a new environment. As he does not know how to drink coffee, he orders a pack of Parle Milk biscuits and tea. But, soon, he finds that the people who were pouring coffee and drinking it in different ways were new and taking coffee for the first time. It sounds positive for him because no one will notice him as "the city was full of outsiders" (296). He observes the people and their ways, and comes to conclusion that outsourcing is the only field that can give "real estate, wealth, power, sex" and, hence, makes up his mind to join it in one way or another. He goes to a Toyota Qualis dealer and asks for the cars on rent. With the money of his master Mr Ashok, he begins his journey of driving technology forward and becomes Ashok Sharma, a North Indian entrepreneur. A halwai who was supposed to be a sweet-maker now writes his own fate by becoming an entrepreneur.

He maintains his 150-square-foot office with chandeliers. Life in Bangalore seems to be good because of "rich food, beer, nightclubs" (13). But, he does not like the Bangalore attitude and the people whom he calls "animals" (54) because of their living. He tells the Chinese Premier about the people of Bangalore thus: "See, men and women in Bangalore live like the animals in a forest do. Sleep in the day and then work all night, until two, three, four, five o'clock, depending, because their masters are on the other side of the world, in America" (298). He considers the time 2:44 a.m. as "the hour of degenerates, drug addicts—and Bangalore-based entrepreneurs" (91). This is the city where the health minister and the chief minister announce the elimination programmes—of malaria and malnutrition respectively. With his money, he purchases the policemen. He calls them paunchy men who become his men. They can be found "swinging their canes on Brigade Road, poking and harassing vendors and shaking them down for money" (300). He walks early in the morning or in the evening only to listen to the road and the pavement with which he never likes to lose contact. He also expects from others to keep ears open so that they may hear "stirrings, rumours, threats of insurrection" (303) and to join together to "destroy the Rooster Coop" but doubts because of the occurrence of the revolution once in a hundred year.

Bangalore is a city of light—the light of technology which will give the power to rule. But, this light, no doubt, has given the light of comforts but it has darkened man's soul. Man simply has turned into a robot with a brain. Here, to think everyone "moral and upright" is not true as if the city has "its share of thugs and politicians" (306). But, what is good here is that it provides a man choice—the choice that he did not find in Laxmangarh. "It's just that here, if a man wants to be good, he *can* be good" (306). Now, he has become a rich man and so does not go to the red light districts but loves to buy the girls from five-star hotels. He thinks that "it's not right to buy and sell girls who live in bird cages and get treated like animals. I only buy girls I find in five-star hotels" (304).

There was a time when Balram Halwai used to have a passion for golden-hair girls. Now, he is sick of them because Bangalore is full of these golden-hair foreigners. He plans to work in the construction work but in the end he thinks of selling everything so that he may start a school, "an English-language school—for poor children in Bangalore" (320). Through this school, he wishes to prepare white tigers with the facts of life and plans to unleash them in Bangalore so that he may become the boss. He loves to live in Bangalore because of choice. It is the choice that makes the difference. But in Laxmangarh, a man "doesn't even have this choice. That is the difference between this India and that India: *Choice*" (306). The five-stars hotels of Delhi are even mystery to him but so far as the five-star hotels of Bangalore are concerned, he knows "inside out" because he has spent a lot of money in eating "kebabs of chicken, mutton, and beef" there and enjoying "sluts of all nationalities" (200). The white tiger, after killing the lamb, has become ambitious. That day is not far when he will become the boss of the world. This tiger with the brain is on the move. The brain has crushed his heart. For him, the brain is important because this is the only thing that "a thinking man has in this world" (305).

Credit goes to Adiga who has succeeded in giving spatial identity in *The White Tiger*. He has mentioned the name of the other places but the story of the novel moves around only three places—Laxmangarh, Delhi and Bangalore. He has come out from the place of Darkness to the place of Light. If the river and ocean are taken in perspective of geographical identities, he proves to be wrong because he has mentioned only the dark area and forgets to mention the area which has become alive materially as well as spiritually because of the river. It is not necessary that all the places that are near the ocean are well-off. If he sees the map of India, many places near the ocean are still dark regarding the standard of life. But, he seems to be talking of light and dark in reference to technology. It is certain that the countries rich in technology will dominate the countries either of less technology or no technology. What India needs is advanced technology. This technology is needed even in turning the villages into high-tech villages. This is the other aspect that needs more clarification and discussion. But, regarding, the topography, Adiga has attempted to give the feel of the particular place which he has mentioned. Every place—be it Laxmangarh or Delhi or Bangalore—is given its own spatial identity. But, these places are observed from the specs of a half-baked Indian, the qualification of being an entrepreneur for Adiga, not from a full-baked Indian who is supposed to wear a nice suit and serve throughout life. Hence, to generalise that this is India with its topography is a biased view. This is the fragmentary view of the landscapes, not the full view that needs not the driver's jaundiced eyes that see the things in flashes but the healthy eyes of a true Indian who considers the land as his motherland.

Work Cited

Adiga, Aravind. *The White Tiger*. New Delhi: HarperCollins, 2008. **Print.**

13

The Narrative Configurations

The way Aravind Adiga's *The White Tiger* roars hypnotises the readers whc hear its forceful roaring silently with hands on their hearts and curiosity mixed with mystery in their minds. But, what this tiger roars becomes a matter of concern for the Indians. 'How' dominates 'what' in Adiga's jungle where the tiger is left for roaming while roaring and roaring while roaming. The roar is heard all over the world and the West books *The White Tiger* for the Booker Prize which provides a multimedia system for its roaring so that it can be heard everywhere. The place of nation has been taken by narration. The narration opens the nation's body through the Western knife and displays its rotten parts which are being sold in the global market like hot cakes.

Adiga has succeeded in keeping everyone silent regarding his narrative configurations. Anyone who interrogates the relevance of the Booker Prize for *The White Tiger* cannot help him without appreciating it for its narrative techniques. The novel is a mockery of the upper class, of religion and of traditional values. What makes Adiga appealing is the way that he deals with the tonal variations. The narration is terrific but its authenticity is in peril in spite of his attempt to articulate different voices with a different approach. In the novel, the plot is not complicated as it does not create any suspense. The reader already comes to know beforehand about the murder that will take place later. Balram Halwai is the protagonist of *The White Tiger* who narrates the story of his entrepreneurship. His journey from innocence to experience starts from Laxmangarh and reaches its end in Bangalore via Delhi.

The White Tiger, epistolatory in spirit, begins with the letter that he writes to His Excellency Wen Jiabao who is on his mission to India to know the truth about Bangalore. He offers his service in letting him know the truth through the story of his life. The novel begins thus:

> For the Desk of:
> His Excellency Wen Jiabao,
> The Premier's Office,
> Beijing,
> Capital of the Freedom-Loving Nation of China
>
> From the Desk of:
> 'The White Tiger'
> A Thinking Man
> And an entrepreneur
> Living in the world's centre of technology and outsourcing
> Electronics City Phase 1 (just off Hosur Main Road),
> Bangalore, India.
>
> Mr Premier,
> Sir.
> Neither you nor I speak English, but there are some things that can be said only in English. (4)

Right from the beginning, the novel makes an emotional bond with the reader who is interested in reading the letters. Adiga uses such words 'for' and 'from' to give it a genuine flavour and ends the novel making the readers spellbound with the story of his protagonist. The novel ends thus:

> Yours for ever,
> Ashok Sharma
> The White Tiger
> Of Bangalore
>
> boss@whitetiger-technologydrivers.com (321)

Adiga who has recommended the area of light because of technology provides the email ID so that the reader may feel one with him and interact if he has any curiosity though the protagonist asks the Chinese Premier (also the reader) to visit his website to verify what he has said is correct.

The title of the novel is itself a symbol that reveals individuality, power and freedom. Here is the description of how Balram Halwai gets the title 'The White Tiger'.

> The inspector pointed his cane straight at me. 'You, young man, are an intelligent, honest, vivacious fellow in this crowd of thugs and idiots. In any jungle, what is the rarest of animals—the creature that comes along only once in a generation?'
>
> I thought about it and said:
>
> 'The white tiger.'
>
> 'That's what you are, in *this* jungle.'
>
> Before he left, the inspector said, 'I'll write to Patna asking them to send you a scholarship. You need to go to a real school—somewhere far away from here. You need a real uniform, and a real education.'
>
> He had a parting gift for me—a book. I remember the title very well: *Lessons for Young Boys from the Life of Mahatma Gandhi*.
>
> So that's how I became the White Tiger. (35)

Balram who responds to the school inspector well differentiates him from a crowd of idiots. The reply that it is the white tiger that comes only once in a generation shows the seeds of his ambition that later takes the monster form, resulting in the story of stealing and murder. The white tiger cannot be caged; the whole jungle becomes his area. The tiger is white and white is the colour of power—the power which makes him hungry for wine, wealth and women. The inspector thinks that he needs real education and for this he promises to write to Patna for scholarship. But, neither the inspector writes (there is no mention) nor does Balram go to school after the lizard episode and the bonded labour. School is there where Balram is. He makes his own school of which he is the teacher as well as the student. He learns through eavesdropping. Somehow, the school inspector recognises his genius and the potential, and so gives the book on Mahatma Gandhi as a parting gift. When Balram goes to Delhi and later in Bangalore for final settlement, he follows Gandhi not in spirit but in paper currency which makes him available for more cash and fresh flesh. Hence, the white tiger as a metaphorical symbol runs in the jungle of 321 pages right from the beginning to the end. Besides the white tiger, Adiga has exploited the metaphor of rooster coop that equally becomes significant. This is the rooster coop—the coop of the Indian family and adverse circumstances—that the white tiger breaks and becomes free because of his love for identity.

Adiga's career as a journalist equips him with a journalistic mode of writing. The journalistic touch, though he attempts to avoid it, appears in the text. The wanted poster and information in FIR are purely journalistic in nature. Here are the two excerpts about Balram Halwai, the murderer:

> Assistance Sought in Search FOR MISSING MAN
>
> General Public is hereby informed that the man in the picture namely Balram Halwai alias MUNNA son of Vikram Halwai rickshaw-puller is wanted for questioning. Age: Between 25 and 35. Complexion: Blackish. Face: Oval. Height: Five feet four inches estimated. Build: Thin, Small. (12)

and:

> ...any person having any information or clue about this missing man may kindly inform at CBI Web site (http://cbi.nic.in) e-mail ID (diccbi@cbi.nic.in), Fax No. 011-23011334. T No. 011-23014046 (Direct) 011-23015229 and 23015218 Extn. 210 and to the undersigned at the following address or telephone number or numbers given below.
>
> DP 3687 / 05
>
> SHO—Dhaula Kuan, New Delhi
>
> Tel: 28653200. 27641000 (39)

But the journalistic touches make the novel easy to read and also gripping for the readers who are accustomed to the English newspaper.

Adiga has employed a new technique but it is neither a parenthesis (it is not in between a sentence) nor a part of the running text. It is also not a supplement to complete the running idea. It is better called the bracket technique that he uses for his observation and comments. Here are the two excerpts that take the reader peep into the mind of the protagonist for further exploration:

> (For this land, India, has never been free. First the Muslims, then the British bossed us around. In 1947 the British left, but only a moron would think that we became free then.) (21-22)

and:

> (By the way, Mr Premier: have you noticed that all four of the greatest poets in the world are Muslim? And yet all the Muslims you meet are illiterate or covered head to toe in back burkas or looking for buildings to blow up? It's a puzzle, isn't it? If you ever figure these people out, send me an e-mail.) (40)

Adiga also becomes poetic in his description. The text becomes a river where the words become images and symbols that transport the reader to the world of imagination. Here is the prose text illustrated in poetic form to give the impression of the poetic flow in the novel.

> See,
> this country,
> in its days of greatness,
> when it was the richest nation on earth,
> was like a zoo.
> A clean, well-kept, orderly zoo.
> Everyone in his place,
> everyone happy.
> Goldsmiths here Cowherds here.
> Landlords there.
> The man called a Halwai made sweets.

> The man called a cowherd tended cows.
> The untouchable cleaned faeces.
> Landlords were kind to their serfs.
> Women covered their heads with a veil
> and turned their eyes to the ground
> when talking to strange men.
> And then,
> thanks to all those politicians in Delhi,
> on the fifteenth of August, 1947
> the day the British left
> the cages had been let open;
> and
> the animals had attacked and ripped each other apart
> and jungle law replaced zoo law.
> ...
> in the old days
> there were one thousand castes and destinies in India.
> These days,
> there are just two castes:
> Men with Big Bellies,
> and Men with Small Bellies.
> And
> only two destinies:
> eat—or get eaten up. (63-64)

The lines, when placed in poetic form, become the lines of a poem that takes the reader first to the old days and then bring them to the present day offering him an alternative to make comparison between the two. Adiga is indeed praiseworthy for making the prose poetic and giving it a continuous flow. He is a past master in the use of similes and metaphors. It seems that the poet has entered him and taken the pen from him to write the figures. The figures are rich in conception as they have the potential for further elaborations. Here are some instances of the use of similes:

> A rich man's body is like a premium cotton pillow, white and soft and blank (26)
>
> Like eunuchs discussing the Kama Sutra, the voters discuss the elections in Laxmangarh (98)
>
> 'Mastering a car'—he moved the stick of an invisible gearbox—'it's like taming a wild stallion (56)
>
> The lion and the lioness were apart from each other and not talking like a true city couples (276)
>
> After showing it to me, Vitiligo-Lips closed the magazine and threw it into the circle where the other drivers were sitting; they made a grab for it, like a bunch of dogs rushing after a bone. (126)

The White Tiger possesses the ingredients of a drama like conflicts and dialogues. Dialogues reveal the conflict as well as the information that helps in forwarding the story to its final goal. Adiga has inserted a few dialogues in the text. Mark the two excerpts for the nature of dialogues:

> The old driver asked, 'What caste are you?'
>
> 'Halwai.'
>
> 'Sweet-makers,' the old driver said, shaking his head. 'That's what you people do. You make sweets. How can you learn to drive?' (56)

and

> 'Do you drink?'
>
> 'No, sir. In my caste, we never drink.'
>
> 'Halwai...' Mr Ashok said with a grin. 'Are you a sweet-maker? Can you cook for us while you're not driving?'
>
> 'Certainly, sir. I cook very well. Very tasty sweets. *Gulab jamuns*, *laddoos*, anything you desire,' I said. 'I worked at a tea shop for many years,'
>
> Mr Ashok seemed to find this amusing. 'Only in India,' he said. 'Your driver can also make sweets for you. Only in India. Start from tomorrow.' (65)

The first excerpt is the dialogue between the old driver and Balram. The old driver is not sure of Balram's skill in learning driving. This dialogue gives a peep into the mind of the old driver who is traditional in outlook and thinks that a halwai can make sweet but cannot learn driving. The second excerpt is the dialogue between Mr Ashok and Balram. Balram who has come for the job of a driver again is interrogated regarding his caste. Here again he is supposed to make sweets besides driving.

Balram Halwai imagines the thing because of his apprehensive brain. Adiga has given this quality to his protagonist who begins to think while concentrating on the issue. This habit gives him a way out of a difficult situation and sometimes makes him afraid to the extent that he does not take decisions. In the end, when he reads a story of the mass murder of a family of 17 members, he imagines his family. His mind begins to imagine so much that he does not read the newspaper for a few months. Here is an excerpt that displays the inner working of Balram's mind when Mr Ashok and Mr Mukesh interrogate him regarding caste and family:

> He must have phoned his man in Laxmangarh. And then that man must have gone and spoken to Kusum, and asked the neighbours about us, and phoned back: 'He's got a good family. They've never made any trouble. Father died some years ago of TB. He was a rickshaw-puller. Brother is in Dhanbad too, a worker in the tea shops. No history of supporting Naxals or other terrorists. And they don't move about: we know *exactly* where they are. (66)

Such imagining apprehensiveness makes the reader imagine the case and feel it as his own. Besides, imagining apprehensiveness, Adiga makes Balram use the technique of 'Aside' so that he may calculate the reality and form his point of view. When Pinky Madam goes away leaving Ashok alone, he becomes frustrated to the extent that he thinks that it is useless to be alive. Then, Balram, while speaking to Mr Ashok, also imagines the answer in his mind but does not say what he actually thinks or says in his mind about the particular question. Here is an excerpt that illustrates the use of 'Aside' by Balram:

> 'Sometimes I wonder, Balram. I wonder what's the point of living. I really wonder...'
>
> *The point of living? My heart pounded. The point of your living is that if you die, who's going to pay me three and a half thousand rupees a month?* (186)

The White Tiger can also be called a dramatic monologue in the sense that the protagonist Balram speaks but imagines that the Chinese Premier is listening to him. No doubt, he writes letters but thinks that he is narrating his life story to him. But, sometimes, Adiga uses the inner monologues which come close to soliloquy. When Balram Halwai drops Pinky Madam at the airport, she gives him a brown envelope. He opens it and finds forty-seven hundred rupees. He wonders why she has given this odd sum of money. He begins to talk to himself to find out the possible answer:

> Forty-seven hundred rupees. In that brown envelope under my bed.
>
> Odd sum of money—wasn't it? There was a mystery to be solved here. Let's see. Maybe she started off giving me five thousand, and then, being cheap, like all rich people are—remember how the Mongoose made me get down on my knees for that one-rupee coin?—deducted three hundred.
>
> *That's not how the rich think, you moron. Haven't you learned yet?*
>
> She must have taken out ten thousand at first. Then cut it in half, and kept half for herself. Then taken out another hundred, and anther hundred. That's how cheap they are.
>
> *So that means they really owe you ten thousand. But if she thought she owed you ten thousand, then what she truly owned you was, what—ten times more?* (206)

What makes Aravind Adiga a different tiger is his acute and minute observation and the way of presentation. It is communicative skill that fertilises the seeds of observation resulting in the trees laden with fruits in the mind of the reader who enjoys the genuine taste. Mark the excerpt for Adiga's minute observation of the cockroaches and their activities:

> The second night, I did not sleep in the dormitory—I went to the room. I swept the floor, tied the mosquito net to four nails on the wall, and went to sleep. In the middle of the night, I understood why the mosquito net had been left there. Noises woke me up. The wall was covered with cockroaches, which had come to feed on the minerals or the limestone in the plaster; their chewing made a continuous noise, and their antennae trembled from every spot on the wall. Some of the cockroaches landed on top of the net; from inside, I could see their dark bodies against its white weave. I folded in the fibre of the net and crushed one of them. The other cockroaches took no notice of this; they kept landing on the net—and getting crushed. Maybe everyone who lives in the city gets to be slow and stupid like this, I thought, and smiled, and went to sleep. (131)

Adiga who has dipped his pen in the satirical ink writes the simple words with antithetical meanings. Irony is the weapon that he uses with great ability. He satirises pungently but uses the indirect manner. Here lies the irony of expression. Mark the excerpt for the satirical vein:

> The police know exactly where to find me. They will find me dutifully voting on Election Day at the voting booth in the school compound in Laxmangarh in Gaya District, as I have done in every general, state, and local election since I turned eighteen.
>
> I am India's most faithful voter, and I still have not seen the inside of a voting booth. (102)

The use of simple words makes the lines appealing and within understanding but reflection over them reveals a satire on the voting system. Fake voting is revealed here with the help of positive words. This is the magic that only Aravind Adiga can do. The description: "a framed portrait of the god of gods a grinning Mahatma Gandhi" (310) does not reveal Balram's respect for Gandhi but for the notes with his image.

Adiga has interwoven wit and humour in the fabric of *The White Tiger*. It is indeed difficult to maintain the seriousness along with fun touched with wit. The novel is a serious comedy by virtue of its reflection on the predicament of life along with the entertainment that makes one light and relaxed. When Mr Ashok becomes so hopeless that he does not believe in God, Balram Halwai tries to make him laugh so that he may feel the desire to live.

Balram's endeavour to make Mr Ashok laugh succeeds but he does it at the cost of religion. Balram's poster with the two terrorists creates humour.

Adiga who has shown mastery over language likes to use simple words with rich effect. He has sharpened his language with the chisel to give it a proper shape. He uses a short sentence where a long one is not required. He italicises some words to emphasize his point. He uses a phrase or even a word or two in preference to a sentence. Superficiality does not grow in the fictional ground of Adiga who always has scissors or tools that either prune or remove the unnecessary weeds.

Adiga takes the reader into confidence to make them comfortable. He even talks in an informal way to remove the reader's hesitation. He seems to be talking with the reader who begins to flow with him in the narration. Question tags give the reader a personal feeling that binds him with the characters. Here are some instances of question tags and questions:

> Everyone goes to Mumbai in the films after they kill someone, don't they? (297)
>
> 'Everyone has whisky in their car in Delhi, Ashok, didn't you know this?' (213)
>
> Do we loathe our masters behind a facade of love—or do we love them behind a facade of loathing? (187).
>
> But what is the use of winning a battle when you don't even *know* that there is a war going on? (284)

As Adiga is writing a story of Balram, an Indian, he uses some words of Hindi which suggest the fragrance of the Indian ground. *Namaste* (4), goddess Lakshmi (8), *sadhus* (15), *ghat* (16), *daal, rotis* (33) *gulab jamuns, laddoos* (65) *Namaz* (110) *Oooooom* (189) *lassi* (238) *tack, tack, tack* (107) *pucca* (129) *beedis* (265) *paan* (251) are some Hindi words that give the novel an Indian touch. He uses "cousin sister" (36), not cousin as generally in India, people use the word sister or brother with cousin. Phrases like "a slab of flesh" (26), "a busload of men in khaki" (39), "the lucky bastards" (55), "an ammonia break" (202), "a pyramid of middle-class flesh" (27), "immense pyramids of shit" (255) and "stained arse to the stained sky of Delhi" (261) are the instances of Adiga's fresh and innovative phrases that make him unique. But, he has also used some words that cannot be understood by a common man. Here lies his authenticity in peril. How can a villager like Balram who is half-baked because of his incomplete education use the words like "sluts" (200) for a promiscuous woman, "beak" (31) for penis, "arse" (8) for anus and "balls" (237) for testicles, "boobs" (145) for breast, "tummy" (21) for stomach and "piss" (202) for urination? Where has he read about Harry Potter, James Hedley Chase, Khalil Gibran, Adolf Hitler, Desmond Bagley (205)? How does he know about the book "The Joy of Sex" (206)? Even, the language that Adiga has used shows that it is the language not of a villager but of a man who lives in a posh area. He does his best in using short sentence when he shows either an illiterate man or a common man but cannot continue it for a long time because of his mindset that longs for words rich in meanings.

Adiga has turned the novel into poetry because of his technique of dramatic monologue. The way he confesses before the Chinese Premier reminds one of the narration of the Ancient Mariner. Adiga makes his protagonist Balram think too much, so that sometimes one wonders whether he is a driver or an educated man expert in philosophical subjects. No one can deny the gripping influence that the novel has on the mind of the reader.

Going through the text of *The White Tiger*, the reader feels spellbound because sometimes he himself becomes a poet, sometimes finds himself in the theatre watching the drama and sometimes seems to attend a conference where he offers his comments and observations. The Ancient Mariner Aravind Adiga hypnotises the Guest Reader who has no other option except swallowing the story, but when the process of digestion begins, his stomach churns to the extent that he vomits because of the matter dished out to him through narrative configurations.

WORK CITED

Adiga, Aravind. *The White Tiger*. New Delhi: HarperCollins, 2008. **Print.**

14

An Incomplete Truth

An author who works to mutilate the cultural plant for some gains in the name of its future survival cannot be genuine. It is true that "wounds cannot be cured without searching". But, to declare 'deceased' without curing wounds leaves a question mark on the doctor's integrity. This is the same case with Aravinda Adiga, who, while wearing Dickensian garb, declares India a corpse being eaten by the worms of corruption and injustice from inside. Wearing the cloak of a priest does not make a man religious. A Dickensian garb without having the Dickensian spirit does not make Adiga a Dickens. The dual citizenship and the Western upbringing offer him two faces which he often changes from time to time.

The truth about 'White man's burden' is not hidden now. Adiga's plea that he wrote *The White Tiger* with the reformative zeal is another so-called Westernised Indian's burden. 'The White Man's Burden', the old wine has been filled in a new bottle with a new brand, titled, "The Westernised Indian's burden for the greater process of self-examination" so that Indians may enjoy the pleasures of two Indias in one India and feel proud of themselves for being known as 'Other'. His attempt to display India's "brutal injustice of society" for the qualification of being 'Other' on the global stage is really praiseworthy and the West has done its duty faithfully by offering him the Booker Prize for this noble deed.

To call gods 'arses', the Ganga 'the black river', family 'a rooster coop', parliamentary democracy 'a hurdle in catching up with China', voters 'eunuchs', Delhi 'a crazy city with good roads but with bad people', the people of Bangalore 'animals', elections 'disease', muslims 'illiterate', Tamils 'negroes' etc., is not an attack on the country but a dissection necessary for self-examination.

Adiga, the doctor operates the Indian system with the Western tools on the Western table to show the Indian rottenness but knowingly forgets or intends to have no knowledge of the treatment of the post-operational stage. The West has taught him how to operate and not how to treat. Murder the master, steal his money and settle down in a city to be a big entrepreneur alias a white tiger. Adiga has followed what he has written. Dissect India in the name of self-examination, leave her naked on the Western operation table, go to the West for remuneration in the form of Booker Prize and be tagged as "Flaubert, Balzac and Dickens". This is the new mantra of success followed by Aravind Adiga who has done a kind work for India so that she may transform herself into a better society.

Adiga's case seems to be a case of five blind men who touched a part of the elephant and thought the part to be a whole. The elephant was a winnow to him who touched the ear, a snake to him who touched its trunk, a rope to him who touched its tail, a rock to him who touched its side and a pillar to him who touched its leg. No one was right in their description. With the Western black specs, Adiga sees everything black in India and touches only a part of the Indian reality without taking the whole India into consideration. India which is known as Hindustan or Bharat is not simply a country but Bharat Mata, the mother who has fostered a continuous and uninterrupted civilisation "for about five thousand years of known and partly recorded history".

India is not simply a geographical land. It is much more than that. Assimilation and synthesis are her two virtues that make her alive despite many races, tribes, languages, religions and creeds. Cultural synthesis is in her blood. The Himalayas that protect her are the abode of God. The Sun kisses her eastern part first. The river Ganga becomes the Mother Ganga because of her religious significance. The Indian Ocean washes her feet. She was the golden bird before the British invasion.

This is the land where people like Buddha, Nanak, Kabir, Gandhi, were born. Spirituality is her life-breath. Yoga is her strength. The figure of the cosmic dance of Shiva is her symbol that reveals the concept of creation, preservation and destruction. Her contribution in the field of algebra, trigonometry and calculus cannot be forgotten. Zero is her gift. She gave birth to people like Bhaskaracharya who calculated time even before the astronomer Smart, and Budhayana who calculated the value of 'pi'. Ayurveda is her boon to the people for making their life healthy and pleasurable. There was something in her that forced great personalities like Max Muller and Albert Einstein to acknowledge her contribution to knowledge in every field. But, Adiga fails to see and appreciate her illumining aspects because of the dark black Westernised glasses which either give him a false view of the whole India or focus his eye on her rotten democratic system that oozes poverty, injustice and corruption. The Indian family system that joins the people in an emotional bond seems to be a rooster coop that checks the individual growth.

Though Aravind Adiga's protagonist Balram Halwai, does not speak English, he likes to say in English that India is moral and saintly not because of the truth but of the mask worn by the prime minister and his distinguished sidekicks. He considers himself 'tomorrow' and admires China because of its freedom loving spirit. He forecasts that "the future of the world lies with the yellow man and the brown man" (5). For him, the Chinese are ahead of India in every way except entrepreneurship while India, though full of entrepreneurs, fails to provide the basic amenities like drinking water, electricity, proper sewage system, transportation etc. to her citizens. For him, India is a country where the sense of hygiene is absent, discipline is not followed, courtesy is missing and punctuality has lost its way.

In India, a guest becomes a *devta* (*athithi devo bhavo*) but Adiga's fails to find the courtesy in Indians. Mockingly he begins the story of his life by kissing the arse of some god. Calling gods 'arses' is too much. Not to talk of a theist, even an atheist will never call gods 'divine arses'. For Balram, these

36,000,004 divine arses (the number includes one Muslim, three Christian and 36,000,0000 Hindus gods) "seem to do awfully little work—much like our politicians—and yet keep winning re-election to their golden thrones in heaven year after year" (8). He mocks and commits a blasphemous act but daringly declares: "That's not to say that I don't respect them, Mr. Premier! Don't you ever let that blasphemous idea into your yellow skull" (8). He does not feel any shame in stating that his country has double standards. Mark the excerpt that reveal Adiga's denigrating mode: "My country is the kind where it pays to play it both ways : the Indian entrepreneur has to be straight and crooked, mocking and believing, sly and sincere, at the same time" (8-9). To him, every Indian entrepreneur seems to have double standards.

Balram belittles India and holds "glorious parliamentary democracy" responsible for "the whole tragedy to this country" (10) in producing the half-baked people like him and thousands of others. The question arises: Are all the people in India half-baked with half-cooked ideas? If they are so, why does the West enrol them for jobs in its companies? He thinks that half-baked people are masters who have the talent of becoming the entrepreneurs while the full-baked people who "after twelve years of school and three years of university, wear nice suits, join companies and take orders from other men" (11) and remain servants for the rest of their lives. What a mockery!

India is a land where people forget to name their children. Is it really so? Everybody knows the truth. But, to Adiga, it is a fact. The protagonist, "born and raised in darkness" (14) has come from Laxmangarh, a place which is just a few miles away from Bodh Gaya—the town where Buddha got enlightenment. He divides India into two—India of Darkness and India of Light on the basis of river and ocean. He tries to make the Chinese Premier understand that "India is two countries in one: an India of Light, and an India of Darkness. The ocean brings light to my country. Every place on the map of India near the ocean is well-off. But the river brings darkness to India—the black river" (14). He abuses but poses that he never abuses anyone. On the one hand, he calls the river Ganga "daughter of the

Vedas, river of illumination, protector of us all, breaker of chain of birth and rebirth" (15) while on the other, the same river becomes the "river of Death, whose banks are full of rich, dark, sticky mud whose grip traps everything that is planted in it, suffocating and choking and stunting it" (15). How can the river of illumination bring darkness to the area where she flows? It is beyond understanding. Perhaps Adiga knows better if he does not intend to play with the religious feelings associated with the pilgrims. He suggests to the Chinese Premier not to take a dip in the Ganga otherwise "faeces, straw, soggy parts of human bodies, buffalo carrion, and seven different kinds of industrial acids" (15) will enter his mouth. He asks him to leave the river Ganga for the American tourists who "come each year to take photographs of naked *sadhus* at Hardwar or Benaras" (15). Adiga knows better than the American tourists the reasons for their coming to the Ganga. Coming to take the photographs of naked *sadhus* from afar after spending a lot of money seems to be ridiculous. The Ganga is the river that gives life-force to the Indians, but to Adiga, she seems to be the river of death.

A genius like Adiga can see the hierarchy system even in deities. Hanuman who is "everyone's favourite god in the Darkness" (19) represents a "shining example of how to serve your masters with absolute fidelity, love, and devotion" (19). He thinks that hierarchy also enslaves the mentality of the people who never think of getting freedom from their status. He demoralises Hanuman associating him with Maruti. Maruti is a car but Adiga has used it in masculine gender only to demean the image of Hanuman who does what his Lord Rama wishes. Mark the excerpt: "Now, the Maruti is a small, simple fellow, a perfect servant to the driver; the moment you turn the ignition key, he does exactly what the driver wants him to" (62). He mocks at religiousness of the villagers who even worship nature.

A man cannot perform an evil deed all of sudden until or unless it is present somewhere in him. But, Balram holds his master Mr Ashok responsible for the evils. When Mr. Ashok returns from America he is an innocent man, but Delhi corrupts him. He gives the plea that when the master has become corrupt, the driver will automatically follow in the footsteps. He states: "Once the master of the Honda City becomes corrupted, how can the driver stay innocent" (197). He seems to be anti-Muslim as all the Muslims whom he meets are illiterate. He is surprised by the fact that all the great poets of the world are Muslims despite the fact of illiteracy among the Muslims.

In India, casteism is a significant factor that determines the status of an individual. If a man writes halwai with his name or is known as a halwai, he is supposed to be a sweet maker. A sweet maker is not expected to drive a car. The old driver says to Balram: "You make sweets. How can you learn to drive" (56)? Only Muslims, Rajputs, Sikhs who have aggression in their blood are fit for driving.

Dowry has turned into the worst disease that India is suffering from. Balram Halwai narrates the description of dowry that his family got during the marriage of his brother Kishan. He states:

> It was one of the *good* marriages. We had the boy, and we screwed the girl's family hard. I remember exactly what we got in dowry from the girl's side, and thinking about it even now makes my mouth fill up with water: five thousand rupees cash, all crisp new unsoiled notes fresh from the bank, plus a Hero bicycle, plus a thick gold necklace for Kishan. (51)

India, once a rich country, is now poor because of the invaders who came to India and plundered her. It is a tragedy that the rich have deposited their black money in the white country. A gap between the rich and the poor has given birth to unemployment. Inequality is on the rise because of the improper distribution of wealth which is centred only in a few hands. People from villages are seen going to the cities to find work. Mark the excerpt for the unemployment among the people:

> Each year, all the men in the village waited in a big group outside the tea shop. When the buses came, they got on—packing the inside, hanging from the railings, climbing onto the roofs—and went to Gaya; there they went to the station and rushed into the trains—packing the inside, hanging from the railings, climbing onto the roofs—and went to Delhi, Calcutta, and Dhanbad to find work. (26)

In India, teachers are involved in corruption on the plea that they do not get salary in time. Hence, the grant meant for free food for children is pocketed by the teacher. Everyone knows but no one blames the teacher as "You can't expect a man in a dung heap to smell sweet" (33). Hospitals are without doctors not because they are not appointed but because they run private clinics by giving one-third salary to the authority. Even the ward boy does not tell about the doctor unless he gets ten rupees. When Balram goes to the hospital with his father, he has to give the ward boy ten rupees to know about the doctor.

Not to talk of the hospital, even the embassies are not free from corruption. One can get wine or golf balls or women or even boys for sex. Again, sample the excerpt that discloses how far corruption has entered even the embassies:

> The scam is this, Country-Mouse. Foreign wine is very expensive in Delhi, because it's taxed. But the embassies get it in for free. They're supposed to drink their wine, but they sell it on the black market. I can get him other stuff too. Does he want golf balls? I've got people in the US Consulate who will sell me that. Does he want women? I can get that too. If he's into boys, no problem. (127)

Bribery in the police department is not new. Anything can be done with the help of bribery. Gandhi is the god of gods. Adiga uses Gandhi not in the sense of honour but to demean his stature confined to bank notes. Balram Halwai bribes the police and gets his work done.

When the roads are blocked and the people with "red head-bands shouting slogans" are seen, one must know that it is election time. India is the largest democracy in the world. Adiga has pointed out that democracy is not a boon to India but a curse that has stopped her vying with China. In India, "the awe-inspiring spectacle of one billion people casting their votes to determine their own future, in full franchise" (95) becomes a hot topic. India is proud of the democratic system. He shares: "we may not have sewage, drinking water, and Olympic gold medals, but we do have democracy" (96). If he is given a chance to make the fate of India, he will "get the sewage pipes first, then the democracy" (96). He comments on the process of adding the names to the voting list. The minimum age is eighteen. Those who do not know their age become 18 for the officers who come to enrol. In India, votes can be bought. Before the election, the tea shop owner has already sold the votes of the people who are working on his shop. Who stands in the election? Election is the worst disease that makes voters "talk and talk about things that they have no say in…Like eunuchs discussing the Kama Sutra" (98).

Vijay, the hero of Balram, is the opportunist who changes his dress from time to time. He quits his old job of a bus conductor, wears a red headband and delivers speeches in support of the Great Socialist party. Booth-capturing also becomes a common scene. How is it possible that everyone votes for the Great Socialist? He tells the Chinese Premier that he is a murderer and the police know where to find him. Some people do not go for voting but the record tells that they have used their voting rights. False or fake voting is reported. Balram has never seen a voting booth but his vote is always used by someone else.

It is the only magic of democracy that can make Stork bow down before Vijay, a pigherd's son, and compel the Mongoose to hold a spittoon for the Great Socialist who spits into it thrice to humiliate him. This humiliation from the Great Socialist also becomes a touchstone that works in his favour for keeping on voting for him each time. In India, election can be managed. Emotional speeches are made to exploit the people of darkness. As soon as the news of the victory of the Great Socialist Party is announced, Mr Ashok is shocked for he thinks that he will never come out from the mess of income-tax.

Adiga thinks that in India everyone is in the rooster coop that has confined the individual, who even tries to come out, cannot do so because it is "guarded from the inside" (194). The rooster coop restrains the liberty and makes him realise the inferior state. To Adiga, "*the Indian family*, is the reason we are trapped and tied to the coop" (176). His protagonist does not talk of the family, rather he is in favour of the destruction of the institution of the family. When he goes to work in the city, he is supposed to send money to the village for the family. Kusum blackmails Balram emotionally saying that it is really tragic that she is working even in old age despite his job. She thinks of his marriage to tame him. Mark the excerpt for the conversation:

> 'My grandson has a job, and he still forces me to work. This is the fate of an old woman in this world.'
>
> 'Marry him off!' the neighbours yelled. 'That's the only way to tame the wild ones like him!' (84)

Again, she writes an emotional letter to tempt him to marry.

> But I tempt you with the joys of married life. It is good for the community. Every time there is a marriage there is more rain in the village. The water buffalo will get fatter. It will give more milk. These are known facts. We are all so proud of you, being in the city. But you must stop thinking only about yourself and think about us too. First you must visit us and eat my chicken curry. Your loving Granny. Kusum.' (190-191)

It is a sad fact that most of the people are in the rooster coop which does not let a servant be dishonest. When Pinky Madam kills a boy in an accident, Balram is asked to take the crime on himself. He will prove himself an ideal example of the perfect servant by going to jail. He does not think of running away from there because of the rooster coop that does not allow such an idea to enter his mind. If he makes the confession before the judges, they will not take care because of their involvement in the racket which makes them take bribe for ignoring the discrepancies in the case.

In India, there is no dictatorship and no secret police because of the presence of the rooster coop. He shares with the Chinese Premier that "Never before in human history have so few owed so much to so many, Mr Jiabao. A handful of men in the country have trained the remaining 99.9 percent—as strong, as talent, as intelligent in every way—to exist in perpetual servitude; a servitude so strong that you can put the key of his emancipation in man's hands and he will throw it back at you with a curse" (175-176). Only a man "who is prepared to see his family destroyed—hunted, beaten, and burned alive by the masters" can think of breaking the rooster coop.

When Balram murders his master Mr Ashok and steals the money, he goes to the station where he weighs himself on the weighing machine which throws a chit on which is written "YOUR WEIGHT 59. Respect for the law is the first command of the gods" (248). Even the machine tries to confine him to the rooster coop at the time when he is on the threshold of his freedom. This happens not only with the servants but also with the women who are treated badly and confined to the rooster coop. Pinky Madam is not in the coop. The Stork scolds Mr Ashok for not controlling his wife better "the way we do it in the village" (180). A divorced man is not respected in the society. Mr. Mukesh asks Mr. Ashok to remarry:

> 'All right. Take your time. But you must remarry. If you stay a divorced man, people won't respect you. They won't respect us. It's the way our society works. Listen to me. Last time you didn't listen, when you married a girl from outside our caste, our religion—you even refused to take dowry from her parents. This time, *we'll* pick the girl.' (239)

To become free, he rejects the values and traditions that chained him to the rooster coop. He enters the Black Fort, reaches the top from where he looks down on the temple tower, the market, water buffalo etc., at Laxmangarh and then spits again and again. His spitting is not simply an act of spitting but spitting on the values and tradition. With Mr Ashok and

Pinky Madam, he goes to Delhi which for him is "a crazy city" (118) where "the roads are good, and the people are bad" (124). It is a city "where civilisation can appear and disappear within five minutes" (281). Here, the people from the darkness live on the sides of the road.

The ancient India seems to Balram a zoo "a clean, well-kept, orderly zoo" (63) but, after freedom, the animals from the cages come out and attack one another resulting finally in jungle law replacing the zoo law. In place of a thousand castes and destinies, the jungle law recognises only two castes "Men with Big Bellies, and Men with Small Bellies" and two destinies "eat or get eaten up" (64). The rich people do not have drivers, cooks, barbers and tailors, rather they have servants who become all-in-one. The rich treat their dogs like human beings and human beings like dogs. The dogs are worth more than the servant. Mr Ashok, who has returned from New York, thinks of settling in India because of the bright future which he sees here. India that is changing with speed is "going to be like America in ten years" (89). He feels comfortable here and people care for him—be they drivers or watchmen or masseurs. Later, Balram, the White Tiger who takes his new avatar as Mr Ashok Sharma (the name of his master whom he killed), thinks of transforming the face of Bangalore turning it into a "decent city, where humans can live like humans and animals can live like animals. A new Bangalore for a new India" (318). He knows that there occurs a revolution to make the poor free but once in a hundred years. Later, he thinks of selling everything to begin a school where he will prepare white tigers whose heads will be free from the ideas of God or Gandhi.

For Adiga, the traffic system is out of order in India. New York is the city where driving is comfortable. So far as driving in India is concerned, it is next to impossible because of the crazy people who do not follow rules. Mr Ashok makes Pinky Madam understand the difference between India and New York concerning traffic rules. He states: "'Pinky, that was New York—you can't drive in India, just look at this traffic. No one follows any rules—people run across the road like crazy—look –look at that" (81). Is it so in India? Has Adiga ever tried to cross the red light either in Delhi or Bangalore? Why does he make Pinky Madam say: "What a fucking joke! Everyone in India drinks and drives. But you won't let *me* do it" (159)? Is every Indian drunkard?

Balram escapes and lives in the light while the police are searching for him in darkness. How does Adiga think that "This is India, not America. There's always a way out here" (121). If it had been so, everyone would have been interested in committing crime. It is surprising that he finds "honesty among thieves" (308). Why does he think that foreigners go to the Himalayas, or to Benaras, or to Bodh Gaya for doing yoga or smoking hashish or shagging a *sadhu*? Are the sadhus homosexual? Why does he suggest to the Chinese Premier to go to the National Zoo in place of the Ganga or ashrams for enlightenment? Why does he think that a murder is necessary to be a man? Why does he consider that "There's no reward for entrepreneurship in most of India" (59)? Is it really true that "free people don't know the value of freedom" (117)? What does freedom mean? Does freedom come only after committing murder? Is Parliamentary democracy a single reason that checks India from competing with China? If not democracy, what is the other form of government that can help India to catch up with China? In villages, Adiga does not find separate rooms for people who "just lie together at night and fuck like that" (190). The Western dark specs make him see everything dark. Even the light becomes dark.

Sometimes, Adiga's pen writes the facts that are true but the next moment, the protagonist reverses the equation. When Pinky Madam leaves Mr Ashok, he feels isolated and alienated and comes to know the importance of family. He states: "But without family, a man is nothing. Absolutely nothing. I had nothing but this driver in front of me for five nights. Now at last I have someone real by my side: you" (189). When the fat man comes to know the divorce of Mr Ashok, he feels sorry to hear and says: "Marriage is a good institution. Everything's coming apart in his country. Families, marriages—everything." (214). But, to the protagonist, all these institutions are part of the rooster coop that stops the growth of a man. Here, the

Indian economy is based on "the trustworthiness of servants" (175). His philosophy that "Let animals live like animals; let humans live like humans" (276) seems good and sound but to recommend one murder to be a man is quite eccentric. If his advice is followed, every servant will take the initiative of murdering his master to be a free man.

It seems that Adiga is himself in the Western rooster coop that has made his conscience prisoner. He is unknown to the conspiracy of the butcher West that has ensnared him mentally in the name of globalisation. Indians under the British rule killed Indians physically. Now, the West has appeared in the pleasing global shape attracting the authors like Adiga so that they may murder their comrades culturally to the extent that they may begin to think themselves as inferior and acknowledge their image of 'Other'.

Adiga cannot dissociate himself on the plea that the novel is a piece of art. The views expressed are not his own but are of various characters expressed in different situations and circumstances. When an author writes—be it an autobiography or a fiction or a poem or a fantasy or anything else—, he cannot make himself free with this plea of impersonality. Parents cannot dissociate themselves from their children because of the separate individuality. Polyphonic voices in fiction are the outcome of one mastermind that manipulates in different ways. But, Adiga who does not care for the Indian feelings makes his protagonist Balram Halwai a Dushashan who pulls the sari of Draupadi India on the global stage.

"Nothing is either good or bad but thinking makes it so" says Shakespeare. A patriot of one's country may be a villain for another country. Adiga is honoured because he has done the right thing for the West. Does he himself feel honoured inwardly? Does his conscience not rebuke him for presenting the incomplete picture of India? How can he live in peace with this incomplete truth or *adhura sach*? Does his heart not long for completing the incomplete picture? Probably his heart cries but remains silent at the next moment because of the rooster coop protected and sponsored by the West which makes him forget to raise his pen in praise of India. He makes his protagonist interested in dipping his 'beak' into a virgin that can cure any disease—be it of body or mind. What a prescription from this Westernised Indian doctor who intends to take out the cultural uterus from the body of mother India in the name of the process of self-examination! Mark one excerpt from the text when Balram is confused and does not know what to do:

> Completely confused by the time, I compromised—I took the car five feet in front of the white line, and then came to a stop.
>
> 'Did you see what he did?' Mr Ashok said. 'That was pretty clever.'
>
> 'Yes, Ashok. He's a fucking genius.' (160)

Balram compromises and drives the car up to the five feetmark in front of the white line. This action makes Ashok and Pinky Madam recognise his genius in keeping their words. Pinky Madam calls him "a fucking genius". What she says about Balram is true for Adiga who very cleverly presents the dark story in an engrossing manner mixed with entertainment, a technique that keeps the reader fully awake up to the end of the novel. No doubt, Raina in Shaw's *Arms and the Man* speaks in a thrilling voice and Bluntschli appreciates her for this but does not believe in what she says. What Adiga tells in *The White Tiger* partially may or may not be true but the way he narrates is fascinating. He has dipped his pen in the ink that contains irony, paradox and satire as ingredients. But, the message which his *The White Tiger* conveys seems to be unrealistic as it will lead the country to the road of anarchism. Murder, steal and be the entrepreneur. If all the people follow the dictum, what will happen? Will India be on the road of global harmony? Is he really a messiah of the *dalits*? Can crime really result in the prosperity of India? Where will Adiga lead the Indians after mutilating their cultural ethos? How far do novelists like Adiga hurt the national pride by exposing the poverty and injustice on the global platform? Is the West free from evils? How far will Adiga see the superficial view of India with the Western specs? The West may believe in Balram

Halwai's story but one day, God will come to take him to His Court where he will complete the incomplete truth. The robotic atheistic white tigers from the school where no one is allowed to corrupt his head with the stories about God and Gandhi will fail to save this boss of Bangalore from the clutches of the boss of bosses—God. "Time is up, Munna."

Work Cited

Adiga, Aravind. *The White Tiger*. New Delhi: HarperCollins, 2008. **Print.**